From Battlefield to Bottom Line

Also by Bil Holton

From Battlefield to Boardroom:
The Leadership Lessons of Robert E. Lee

From
Battlefield to Bottom Line

The Leadership Lessons of Ulysses S. Grant

Bil Holton, Ph.D.

PRESIDIO

Published by Presidio Press
505 B San Marin Drive, Suite 300
Novato, CA 94945-1340

Library of Congress Cataloging-in-Publication Data

Holton, Bil.
    From battlefield to bottom line : the leadership lessons of
Ulysses S. Grant / Bil Holton.
    p.   cm.
    Includes bibliographical references.
    ISBN 0-89141-579-3 (pbk)
    1. Grant, Ulysses S. (Ulysses Simpson), 1822–1885—Quota
tions. 2. Leadership—Quotations, maxims, etc. I. Title.
E672.H8   1995
973.8'2—dc20   95-30927
                                          CIP

Printed in the United States of America

CONTENTS

Preface   ix
Acknowledgments   xi
Introduction   xiii
Grant's Leadership Lessons   1
Endnotes   149
Bibliography   151

PREFACE

For the past twenty-four years, my leadership and teambuilding consultancy has taken me into the world of the human side of quality. I have been in the company of some of the greatest scientists, sages, presidents, educators, management gurus, sports coaches, political leaders, and military officers this century has produced. My association with such an elite group of leaders has been humbling, inspiring and, at times, riveting.

I am convinced that there are qualities and attributes inherent in leadership that demand serious attention and scholarly investigation. The magic of the "mix" between leader and circumstance has produced—no, uncovered—leaders of exceptional quality and character. I have been privileged to see people accept the mantle of leadership; and serve their organization, military unit, religious order, school and country heroically. It occurred to me that the world needs to have access to the greatness of such people. In the time when role models of a higher order are needed, there must be, I reasoned, some mechanism to prove to a hungry world that authentic leadership excellence still exists.

From Battlefield to Bottomline evolved out of that concern and growing commitment to provide today's leaders with sage-like leadership wisdom. As I focused my research efforts more on the qualities of great leaders and the crucible of experience through which those qualities emerged, I knew I had to start with heroes from America's past. One of those people was Ulysses S. Grant.

Here was an ordinary man of common stock with uncommon determination and resolve. His meteoric rise to national, then international fame helped him move well beyond the illusion of his own insignificance and proved to the world—and to himself—that there is leadership capacity in all of us. And that is Grant's legacy to anyone who wants to assume the responsibilities of leadership. What emerged was the absolute relevance of Grant.

My journey to uncover Grant, the man; Grant, the leader; Grant, the symbol of every man, took me to places I count as sacred ground, as hallowed ground, as cherished ground, indeed! As my research continued, I was drawn to walk physically through the trenches at Cold Harbor, Fredericksburg and Petersburg. I was transformed, and deepened, as I visited history at Chancellorsville, Saylors Creek, and Yellow Tavern. I heard the shouts of victory ring loudly off the heights of Vicksburg. My eyes moistened as I read the accounts of valor, daring and sacrifice eulogized by historians. I was honored to shake the hand of John Griffiths, the great, great grandson of Ulysses S. Grant.

I have emerged from the research for this book more resolved than ever to polish my craft, to rededicate myself to a more rigorous study—a more open-minded study—of leadership. The art of leadership is a painting constantly in progress. The canvas is the experience, the colors are the leader's personality, track record, and credentials; and the brush is synchronicity which brings leaders and circumstance together at precisely the appointed hour.

ACKNOWLEDGMENTS

A book such as this is the cumulative product of many people, present company and ancestral. It began as a research project a little over two years ago, on the relevance of Ulysses S. Grant's leadership abilities to today's leadership community. I extend immense gratitude to those insightful and patriotic historians who reported the generalcy and uncovered the man we know as U. S. Grant. I am also thankful to his living descendants, in particular to John Griffiths, who permitted my gentle trespass into their lives and their rich American Heritage. In fitting tribute I can say that I witnessed some of the essential high qualities of Grant in his descendants. It appears that his uncommon sense, determination, unassuming nature, practicality, love for America, quiet decency, and tenacity are still very much ingrained throughout his family, in the fabric of America.

For her understanding, incredible patience and love, I owe an eternal debt of gratitude to my wife, Cher. She was a constant source of unruffled composure and unfailing support through the sometimes chaotic, othertimes comatose phases of this project.

Nancy Whitaker's ability to crank out reams of manuscript, interpret my sometimes unintelligible scratch, provide valuable editing support, and catch my occasional redundancy was absolutely heroic. Her genuine interest was matchless. Her care in helping me give birth to this book was affectionate and motherly.

Artistic input was provided by Ted Williams who accented transition points between strategies with artwork.

My publisher was truly a valued partner in rolling out the process from manuscript to book. The author-publisher relationship is part of the product as well, making the whole process productive, efficient and enjoyable.

INTRODUCTION

The question many people have asked me when the nature of this book was announced was: *Why Grant?* The man, his generalcy, and his presidency all conjure up mixed emotions. Ulysses S. Grant was, after all, an average man of character, a general who knew how to run military machinery, yet who fell victim to political machinery as President.

What I found compelling about Grant as the subject of *From Battlefield to Bottomline* was the man himself. My overall impression of the man, public and private, is that he epitomized the "new" America. He was the chief operating officer of an emerging industrial America. My picture of him is that of a rather unassuming man, medium in height, of common stock and certainly not the killing warrior nor the bumbling politician that more unenlightened critics depict. Looks can be deceiving and first impressions of Ulysses S. Grant are definitely deceiving. There is almost no glamour, no pomp and circumstance in his demeanor. He cannot be made into a Wellington or a Napoleon— or a Lee.

There are historians who insist that Grant must have had some secret genius that propelled him toward greatness. Others contend that if he had this greatness, it lay dormant, hidden within him, unknown to Grant and unwitnessed by anyone else. No amount of revision can change the way tens of thousands of men died at Cold Harbor or the fact that the men in The Whiskey Ring embezzled money. But history also records many incidences of a more empathetic Grant, a more humanitarian Grant that the general public has not witnessed. So who was Grant? A lamb or a junkyard dog? A Michaelangelo or a Hitler? A saint or a destroyer? *From Battlefield to Bottom Line* brings the reader enough snapshots of Grant for the reader to judge his worth, as a leader and as a human being.

I have had the privilege of getting to know Ulysses S. Grant through my research which included—and continues to include—my reading, study, interviews and historical site visits. I can honestly say—no, I am absolutely, positively, and completely convinced that Ulysses S. Grant was a great leader and a great American. While he saw himself just a notch above ordinary, he also saw himself embedded in the average. The story of Ulysses S. Grant unfolds the quest of an ordinary, hard-working and decent American making his mark in the mid-nineteenth Century. I sincerely believe his wife, Julia, would agree. He failed as a peacetime army officer, farmer and businessman—yet still wanted to be taken into account. I know his descendants believe that.

So young Sam Grant (that's what his West Point colleagues called him) went to war, as did hundreds of thousands of other unremarkable men cut from pretty much the same mold. Finally, when Grant came into himself—when he began to recognize his growing influence—he took complete command of the war. It became Grant's war, make no mistake about it. The men who fought and died for him were just as trapped in obscurity as he had been—and believed they shared a part of his fame, a glimmer of his success when they gave their lives for him, without fear and without regret. Cheers for Ulysses S. Grant were cheers for their own triumph over adversity and unworthiness.

Grant ranks among those greater souls who have demonstrated exceptional leadership capacity under trying circumstances and in spite of personal failings. Like others he beat the odds. He mastered authority and gained influence. Accomplished what others said could not be done. Knew that the best way to predict the future was to invent it. Managed what he could, when he could, with what he had, and in the end showed the common man and the average woman that they, too, can become leaders not only of people, but of nations.

There is a Grant in each of us. It is the thesis of this book that Grant's leadership and personal qualities, to some degree, are within us. Whether we come from aristocratic or common stock, each of us has a *specialness,* a greatness, that can propel us to the heights of leadership excellence.

Ulysses S. Grant's relentless determination, uncommon sense, humility, resolve, and love of family are qualities that are needed more than ever in a world aching for more civilized leadership. Readers will find a reserved but brilliant Grant. A pragmatic Grant. A global Grant. A Grant that gave the world its first glimpse of an industrial age leader.

From Battlefield to Bottomline is a book that should be kept in the office credenza, at one's bedside, in the study. One to pick up briefly, but reflect on constantly. It is one of those rare books that readers want to revisit often, to dig into, to abstract pearls of wisdom from, to gain hope and help from. Readers—managerial and executive, military and civilian—will find it a wise counselor, a true friend and willing colleague, a book of considerable managerial and leadership guidance.

Every effort has been made to offer the reader a leadership development format that is straightforward, easy to read and substantive. Grant's leadership qualities and personal philosophies are arranged in alphabetical order by topic. Quotes by Grant or about Grant are followed by insightful commentary which draws implications from the material, bringing Grant's wisdom to life for today's leadership community. Readers are encouraged to use the quotes, stories and commentary as *learning ramps* for leadership excellence. Record your own insights in the margins on each page. Note anything that seems especially pertinent to where you are in your journey toward leadership excellence. I believe you will find the time worthwhile. I hasten to add that if you find more Grant-like qualities in your own leadership style than you thought you would, there is only one thing you can do—listen for the cheering, it's for you!

ACCEPTANCE

He was always calm amid excitement, and patient under trials. He looked neither to the past with regret nor to the future with apprehension. What he could not control, he endured.

Horace Porter
Campaigning with General Grant (p. 174)

Acceptance is the triumph of resilience over worry and regret. Leaders who worry over what *might* have been or what *should* have been add insult to injury and difficulties to opportunities. Some leaders see disappointments as temporary setbacks. Others see them as a temporary illness that should be treated like any other sickness. The object is to recover as quickly as possible and get back to the business at hand. Grant had an extraordinary talent for accepting and then enduring what he could not control. Instead of burning up his energy worrying over what might have been, he dug in and focused on his next move.

Grant also knew that once something happened, it was history. It becomes part of the indelible past. As such it cannot be changed, only learned from. Today's leaders can change history by modifying the present—which becomes history soon enough.

ACCOLADES

I am not egotist enough to suppose all this significance should be given because I was the object of it.

U. S. Grant
The Personal Memoirs of
Ulysses S. Grant (p. 666)

James Ford Rhodes, writing of Grant as he became lieutenant general and moved on Virginia, said flatly, "He was now by all odds the most popular man in the United States." George Templeton Strong wrote in his diary, in July, that Grant was "*the* great man of the day—perhaps of the age."

William S. McFeely
Grant: A Biography (p. 169–70)

Displaying honor is much more significant than honors displayed. Accolades, kudos, and praise are all temporary reminders of one's ability to produce them. Unless the motives are right, all public praise and accomplishments turn out to be merely superficial acquisitions of decorative accomplishment. Both praise and censure are external echoes. The chief difference between a pat on the back and a swift kick . . . is simply placement.

ADDICTIONS

Men on the frontier did not take cocktails before dinner, or sip from a snifter with their evening cigar. They drank! At Humboldt . . . Grant . . . drank . . . whiskey . . . without water and he did it every day and often every day.

Gene Smith
Lee and Grant (p. 64–65)

There is no safety from ruin by liquor except by abstaining from it altogether.

U. S. Grant in Gene Smith's,
Lee and Grant (p. 64)

[Rollins] likened Grant to Washington about to cross the Delaware, and declared firmly that "two more nights like the last will find you prostrated on a sick bed unfit for duty." Rollins did not give the letter to Grant, but he did keep it; it was the written version of all the sermons he had imagined directing at this friend whom he took satisfaction in regarding as dependent on him. The friendship of the two was real, and it was important to both; while Rollins may have exaggerated the risk to Grant—and the nation—of his drinking, there is no reason to think him an out-and-out liar. Once again, Grant did drink . . .

Bruce Catton in William S. McFeely's
Grant: A Biography (p. 148)

Upon a few occasions, after a hard day's ride in stormy weather, the general joined the officers of the staff in taking a whiskey toddy in the evening. He never offered liquor of any kind to visitors. The only beverage ever used at the table besides tea and coffee was water . . .

Horace Porter
Campaigning with General Grant (p. 150)

Newspapers told how Grant had been smoking during the battle, and gifts of cigars came in from all quarters—so many that Grant largely gave up his pipe and became a confirmed cigar smoker, if for no better reason than that he had dozens of boxes of cigars lying around headquarters and it seemed a shame to let them go to waste.

Bruce Catton
Grant Moves South (p. 181)

Addictions are more easily broken than mended. Transforming addictions into preferences takes an act of will. Acts of will take resolve. Resolve must be coupled with action, otherwise the addiction remains a self-defeating habit. Addictions are self-rejections fueled by feelings of inadequacy, guilt, and futility. The only safety from ruin is to move beyond the illusion of one's own insignificance.

A sense of dignity and well-being grow with the ability to censor self-defeating habits. These self-imposed habits are defense mechanisms (well-fortified emotional bunkers) that bring lethargy, staleness, and disease.

ANTICIPATION

There is no great sport in having bullets flying about one in every direction, but I find they have less horror when among them than when in anticipation.

U. S. Grant in
William S. McFeely's
Grant: A Biography (p. 32)

Trust only movement. Grant was a permanent resident of the present. He knew that the now, the here, was the place where the future plunged inexorably into the past.

APPROVAL

"I have found in Lieutenant Grant a most remarkable and valuable soldier," Hamer wrote home. "I anticipate for him a brilliant future if he should have an opportunity to display his powers when they mature."

> Tom Hamer, Brig. Gen. of
> volunteers in the Mexican War, in
> Anderson and Anderson's
> *The Generals* (p. 80)

He had no urge to rest on his laurels, which is not to say that he had no taste for the laurels themselves.

> William S. McFeely
> *Grant: A Biography* (p. 103)

Hype, praise, and renown are such yeasty things. As long as you entertain your admirers, they'll keep you puffed up. One false move and they'll burst your manufactured bubble. The greatest accomplishments are usually traced back to the love of praise and the satisfaction produced by notoriety. For some leaders, praise is a well-deserved income. For others, one hiss outweighs uproarious applause. Grant, like still others, earned it and enjoyed it, but never rested his career on laurels, present or past. The only escape, and perhaps the best escape from the personal corruption of hype, praise, and long-drawn-out approval is to go on working. Praise is tough to handle, especially when you stop to listen to it.

AUDACITY

As for Grant, he was like Thor, the hammerer: striking blow after blow, intent on his purpose to beat his way through, somewhat reckless of the cost. Yet he was the first one of our commanders who dared to pursue his policy of delay without apology or fear of overruling. He made it a condition of his acceptancy of the chief command that he should not be interfered with from Washington. That gave him more freedom and "discretion" than any of his predecessors. He had somehow, with all his modesty, the rare faculty of controlling his superiors as well as his subordinates. He outfaced Stanton, captivated the President, and even compelled acquiescence or silence from that dread source of paralyzing power,—the Congressional Committee on the conduct of war.

Joshua Chamberlain
The Passing of the Armies (p. 29)

Audacity is today's rebuttal of yesterday's experience. The men began to realize that this campaign was something special and that they were being led with cold audacity. Grant moved with a growing sense of confidence in the persuasiveness of his record of success coupled with the acquiescence of superiors, who had not figured things out to the point of censoring him. Acquiescence is confirmed desperation. Resignation and desperation will always bow to the punctuality of audacity.

Nevertheless, audacious leaders will have to underwrite their actions with results. Otherwise, enthusiastic gains through such boldness will be met with "paralyzing power" from controlling and watchful superiors.

AUTHENTICITY

His soldiers always knew that he was ready to rough it with them and share their hardships on the march. He wore no better clothes than they, and often ate no better food.

Horace Porter
Campaigning with General Grant (p. 361)

Authenticity invites authenticity. Leaders who are believable unfailingly align attitudes, body language, and principles with actions. For such leaders, authenticity is choreographed character. A touch of genuineness, reliability, and constancy usually accompany authenticity. To attempt to lead without it is to cloak oneself in deceit and pretension. Once contaminated, authenticity is a difficult virtue to resurrect fully, and the offender will always be questioned by distrustful subordinates who feel violated and manipulated. A better return on equity would be to invite authenticity by being authentic. As best you can as a leader and as a human being, stare truth confidently in the face.

BEST PRACTICES

⸻

We had a habit, perhaps, drawn from dire experience, and for which we had also Grant's quite recent sanction (the order to entrench on March 31st on White Oak Road)—when we had carried a vital point or had to hold one, to entrench.

Joshua Chamberlain
The Passing of the Armies (p. 153–54)

Most organizations still require leaders to *handle* people according to mechanistic practices or traditional approaches, as it is referred to today. These traditional *best practices* in terms of managing people fall into three fairly myopic categories: philanthropic, procedural, and protective. They are philanthropic in terms of the desire to attend to the welfare of subordinates (the benefits architecture); procedural in regard to controlling the chores associated with employment (bureaucratic rigmarole); and last, but certainly not least, protective in identifying, preventing, or curing threats to the organization's stability (entrepreneurial people). The best practices in leadership today—and tomorrow—are leading instead of managing and directing processes rather than controlling tasks.

BIAS FOR ACTION

Courage begets energy, but unless a general is bodily and mentally active, unless he is endowed with a will to press on, the energy of courage is apt to effervesce. In war, energy may be, and frequently is misdirected; but even waste of energy is better than lethargy, that unforgivable sin of generalship. Grant's energy is quite extraordinary: fit, or sick, nothing can stop him. He is always ready to act, he is never obsessed by difficulties, he never exaggerates difficulties, or paints mental pictures of imaginary situations.

J. F. C. Fuller
The Generalship of Ulysses S. Grant (p. 190–91)

I was very impatient to get to Fort Donelson because I knew the importance of the place to the enemy and supposed he would reinforce it rapidly. I felt that 15,000 men on the 8th would be more effective than 50,000 a month later.

U. S. Grant
The Personal Memoirs of Ulysses S. Grant (p. 175)

When Grant got to Cruces, he found the rumors were true. Men, women, and children were sickening and dying. . . . Grant leased an old hulk of a boat lying at anchor a mile away from the *Golden Gate* Army transport, moved the ill soldiers and civilians onto this new hospital ship, and volunteered himself for nursing duty when the enlisted men on board deserted. "He was like a ministering angel to us all," one officer wrote, adding that Grant's endurance was amazing. He seldom slept, "and then only two or three hours at a time."

Anderson and Anderson,
The Generals (p. 105)

One *now* is worth two *laters*. This philosophy allows leaders to respond instead of react. No wind favors a commander (or CEO or site manager or department head or anyone else) who is indecisive. The only thing hot air generates is staleness. Oftentimes, "done *now* is better than perfection *later*,"[1] says Cher Holton, Ph.D., management consultant. Determine direction, then move with stealth toward defined objectives. And for heaven's sake, don't try to do anything. To *try* to do something turns out to be a built-in cop-out device employed to cover up lack of commitment, disinterest, indecisiveness, cowardice, or laziness.

BLOWING SMOKE

I have known a few men who were always aching for a fight where there was no enemy near, who were as good as their word when the battle did come.

U. S. Grant
The Personal Memoirs of
Ulysses S. Grant (p. 58)

All excess is excess. Some leaders look good on paper, are decorated with impressive academic credentials, come packaged handsomely in appearance—but it's the word-of-mouth that kills them. Abraham Lincoln knew excess when he saw it: "What kills a skunk is the publicity it gives itself."[2] A little noise proves nothing. Merchandising performance is best done after-the-fact, when the promised performance is met or exceeded.

BREAK THE RULES

Nothing that was not absolutely essential was permitted to be taken ashore to slow [the Federal's] dash at the enemy. General Grant himself took only a comb and a toothbrush—literally. He had no extra clothing, no blanket, not even a horse. He flung his army inland below Vicksburg. Violating the first axiom of war, that troops on the offensive must operate from a base of supplies always covered, Grant had, like Scott advancing upon Mexico City, thrown away precedent. He would live off the land.

Gene Smith
Lee and Grant (p. 151)

He did not wait for Banks to bring his men up from Louisiana to help. Instead, Grant cut his own supply line and imprudently placed his vast army within a pincers formed by Pemberton in Vicksburg and the enemy general Grant most admired, Joseph E. Johnston, northeast of Vicksburg above Jackson, Mississippi. Had Grant's plan failed he would have been pilloried for doing something so stupid, and Johnston was not reluctant to bring on such a punishment.

William S. McFeely
Grant: A Biography (p. 130)

Ignore linearity and discard precedent. Interrupt regularity. Disturb the status quo. Take issue with the processes and means of production. Question everything. Many solutions, as Grant found, lie outside of untested, untried, conventional wisdom. Excursions from normality have helped many leaders turn the corner on bothersome organizational challenges. Such nonconformity and rule-breaking orientation require speculative calisthenics and healthy appreciation for purposeful play to underwrite a successful experience.

Leaders who become comfortable with breaking rules know that there is a relentless gravitational pull toward precedence. This force, this calcified thinking, is counterproductive, particularly since it is so easily justified as conventional wisdom. The following warning is offered unapologetically and without reservation—an organization is dead when its leadership acknowledges only convention.

BREVITY

[The rebels] played it Grant's way. He never mapped strategy, never put pins in charts or moved counters over simulated terrain. Everything was in his head. He heard all that was said around him, he took in every message, he said little. What he wanted people to know he wrote out in his own hand, so there could be no misunderstanding. His crisp, clear orders were almost impossible not to comprehend. Those who did not carry them out either chose not to or lacked any ability to translate words into action.

William S. McFeely
Grant: A Biography (p. 186)

Brevity is compressed verbosity. In the thick of urgent operational realities, it turns out to be the shortest distance between effort and results.

BRIDLED AMBITION

General Grant . . . and the President . . . served [the country] . . . with hearts too great for rivalry, with souls untouched by jealousy, [and] . . . lived to teach the world that it is time to abandon the path of ambition when it becomes so narrow that two cannot walk it abreast.

Horace Porter
Campaigning with General Grant (p. 19)

As Grant shrewdly outmaneuvered potential McClernands and adroitly established his authority over rival generals, he was equally careful to avoid giving any intimations of excessive ambition. Generals like Hooker and McClellan had created great problems for themselves by seeking high positions and the perquisites that accompanied them, but then not matching loftiness with performance on the battlefield. Grant was determined to keep the horse before the cart; he would perform, and then see that what he had done was celebrated.

William S. McFeely
Grant: A Biography (p. 144)

Bridled ambition is spurred complacency. Organizations owe all productivity gains and service distinction to leaders who are ill at ease with the status quo. However, when aspirations become insatiable appetites, tainted by jealousy, and fueled by rivalry, they become pathologically uncontrollable. Such covetousness and gluttony must be checked, or pure unadulterated greed will devour the unsuspecting organization.

Covetous leaders generally use clumsy devices like subtle sabotage, hidden agendas, and character assassinations as stepping stones when they see that the career path is becoming "so narrow that two cannot walk it abreast."

BUREAUCRACY

[Grant's] staff consisted of fourteen officers only, and was not larger than that of some division commanders . . . all the members of the staff had had abundant experience in the field, and were young, active, and ready for any kind of hard work.

Horace Porter
Campaigning with General Grant (p. 30–33)

Trim redundant bureaucracy. When rules, policies, and procedures cease to perform the function they were designed for, modify or eliminate them. Unnecessary rules, policies, and procedures are ballasts that weigh an organization down. Key projects and strategic programs that require cross-functional collaboration are stymied by bureaucratic straitjackets, rigidity, and slowness. Internal groups wage war and departments become so protective of their turf that they refuse to cooperate with anyone they identify as the *enemy*.

Leaders who know about the loose-tight qualities of bureaucracies will enjoy strategic advantages. The most effective leaders are the ones who know how to manage the three contradictions inherent in every organization today: organizations must be global and local, large yet small, and radically decentralized yet centralized in reporting and control. Hierarchies and cross-functional networks of horizontal structures will have to be built and maintained. Hierarchies, bureaucracies, and networks will have to integrate and leverage the strengths of each. What each of these structures looks like will depend on the purpose, the function, the need. With links like these, purpose will pull disparate elements (structures) and act like a centrifugal force. Purpose and function must replace traditional glues such as hierarchical stencils and bureaucratic bottlenecks. Leaders will have to manage this dependence-independence-interdependence balance carefully.

BUSINESS CASUAL

He had ridden more than 35 miles that day over Virginia's muddy springtime roads. He wore the uniform of a private with lieutenant general's stars sewn on. The straps were dingy . . . no sword, no sash, one coat button buttoned in the wrong hole.

> Gene Smith describing Grant's
> appearance at Appomattox
> *Lee and Grant* (p. 269)

He could hear the measured tread of his men, 120,000 strong, moving southeast to look for Robert Lee. Just as the sun was breaking over Fredericksburg . . . He dressed with unusual care that morning. He pulled polished black boots backed with gold spurs over his new blue pants, sashed his uniform coat with silk, and hung a new gold sword around his slim waist. His hat was new, too, black felt and corded with gold. Last, oddly—his staff had never seen him wear them before—Grant put on a pair of buff-colored gloves.

> Anderson and Anderson
> *The Generals* (p. 365)

A comfortable coat seems like an old friend.

> U. S. Grant in Horace Porter's
> *Campaigning with General Grant* (p. 141)

The quiet man, wearing an old jacket, slouching and watching, was thought by fools to be a no-account and was represented by jealous enemies as a drunk. But at the end of Grant's schooling in war, another master at deliberately wearing the wrong clothes, Abraham Lincoln, saw someone very different.

> William S. McFeely
> *Grant: A Biography* (p. 77)

Looks can kill. Self-presentation and personal packaging are essential for perceived credibility. How you are packaged speaks volumes. Your gestures, attitude, and dress must be as choreographed as ballroom dancing and as orchestrated as a symphony. Appearance and dress play influential roles in determining how people judge a leader's worth.

Your public appearance is mass advertising. The better you look the easier it is to sell yourself. After all, advertising is the bait that makes the hook more palatable. Personal advertising through appearance makes the "look" more believable. It establishes a compatibility between looks and power of influence, credibility and performance.

CARBON COPY

Grant the great soldier of no roots whose weakness for liquor was known to the least of his followers, who had risen from nowhere, from failure and griminess and physical labor to do heroic and magical things and to hold out to those who followed him the hope that they too—farmers, laborers, craftsmen, new immigrants—could in America attain great heights, rise in the world, lead men, grow rich, grow famous, become President.

Gene Smith
Lee and Grant (p. x)

Though taciturn in his manner, [Grant] was an amiable man and possessed (as one of Meade's staff officers said) *a rough dignity* . . . he was a professional applying armed might against a people with the simple controlling principle of conquest. This was Grant as a commander, a personification of the forces released for the destruction of the world personified by Lee.

Clifford Dowdey
Lee's Last Campaign (p. 50)

Character is forged in the crucible of experience. It is the product of personality meeting experience. It is the most fundamental credential a leader can possess, because leaders cannot make ideals, ideals make leaders. Perhaps the most valuable consequence of character is the capacity to make yourself do the things you have to do right, when they need to be done, whether you like doing them or not.

CHESSMANSHIP

The formerly all-conquering Grant inevitably reacted to the bungling of his first performance against the Confederacy's hero. But he was not a man to do any repining. He knew the power he had at his command and he knew the limitations of the army he had tangled with. The Army of Northern Virginia had been bolder, more skillful and much fiercer than he had anticipated. Yet Lee's men, catching him at a disadvantage, lacked the strength to drive him from the field, or to impair the effectiveness of the vast and complex organism that was the Army of the Potomac.

Clifford Dowdey
Lee's Last Campaign (p. 172)

Near the Appomattox River, Virginia
Headquarters Armies of the United States
April 7, 1865—5 P.M.
General R. E. Lee,
Comd'g C.S.A.
General: the result of the last week must convince you of the hopelessness of further resistance on the part of the Army of Northern Va. in this struggle. I feel that it is so and regard it as my duty to shift from myself, the responsibility of any further effusion of blood, by asking of you the surrender of that portion of the C. S. Army known as the Army of Northern Va.
Very respectfully, your obt. svt,
U. S. Grant
Lt. Gn.

U. S. Grant in Anderson and Anderson
The Generals (p. 438)

Grant read Lee well [by April 7, 1865]. "There was no pause, no hesitancy, no doubt what to do," his secretary said. "He commanded Lee's army as much as he did ours."

Clifford Dowdey
Lee's Last Campaign (p. 172)

Successful leaders, like successful chess players, know the game and know the opponent's strengths, weaknesses, and idiosyncrasies. Ulysses S. Grant had many advantages over Robert E. Lee in April of 1865, but the principal one was that Grant had escaped Lee, the myth, and dealt with Lee, the man. Because Lee's men "[even when] catching him at a disadvantage, lacked the strength to drive [Grant] from the field" Grant knew the best thing Lee could do was *check* his moves. Grant had "no hesitancy, no doubt" that his opponent would eventually walk into a *checkmate*.

CHIEF OPERATING OFFICER

Meade found [Grant] an *executive man,* whose only place is in the field.

William S. McFeely
Grant: A Biography (p. 158)

The change is evident through a study of [Grant's] dispatches, reports and official correspondence. They become crisper, more solid, straight to the point, business-like; the impression gained by studying them is that of a man who has at last mastered the job of running an army, who no longer doubts either his own status or his own powers and who is moving ahead with full confidence.

William S. McFeely
Grant: A Biography (p. 391–92)

On a very different level, a private soldier got the same impression, saying: "[Grant] will ride along the long line of the army, apparently an indifferent observer, yet he sees and notices everything. He seems to know and remember every regiment, and in fact every cannon in his large army."

Ross A. Webb
Benjamin Helm Bristan:
Border State Politician (p. 115)

Grant would have made a perfect chief operating officer. He loved routine and established tracking and monitoring protocols to ensure compliance. He had "mastered the job of running an army." Persevering and patient, he had his own idea of how long a project—such as a war—should take. He used the weight of his political, economic, and technological machinery to his advantage. He had unusually fine observation skills. As any good operations person, he was able to absorb, remember, manipulate, and manage immense amounts of detail and administrivia. Superdependable and extraordinarily steady and methodical, he always gave a good day's work for a good day's pay.

Good COOs tend to be outstanding at complex and precise work. Usually conservative and orderly in directing movement, they are obsessed with schedules, are thorough, and generally communicate on a need-to-know basis. The good ones, however, have a warrior within them that wants to charge into battle waving copies of the organization's mission statement as a combat insignia. They move people to action and galvanize support quickly by their mere presence on the corporate battlefield. Their very personalities make them leaders "whose only place is in the field."

CIRCUMSTANCES

My idea then was to get through the course [while at West Point], secure a detail for a few years as assistant professor of mathematics at the Academy, and afterwards obtain a permanent position as professor in some respectable college; but circumstances always did shape my course different from my plans.

U. S. Grant
The Personal Memoirs of Ulysses S. Grant (p. 28)

The fact is I think I am a verb instead of a personal pronoun. A verb is anything that signifies to be; to do; or to suffer. I signify all three.

U. S. Grant to John H. Douglas,
his doctor, in William S. McFeely's
Grant: A Biography (p. 516)

To our common eyes it often seems a dark divinity that rules; and the schoolmaster might interchange the verbs.

Joshua Chamberlain
The Passing of the Armies (p. 181)

Leaders (if they are born at all) are born under the weight of circumstances. By sheer determination, leaders can improve less than desirable circumstances. Whatever part they're asked to play, they must play it well. Then, and only then, can leaders move beyond where they are. Successful leaders allow each circumstance to whet their appetites. They soak up the learning. Sponge up the few remnants of wisdom left after each situation abates. Listen to the stirrings of their heart. As one who is leading your organization into the twenty-first century, all a leader has to do is accept the impossible, give up the indispensable, and refuse to submit to intolerable circumstances.

COMMANDING PRESENCE

J. F. C. Fuller quotes Napoleon:

The personality of the general is indispensable, he is the head, he is the all of an army. The Gauls were not conquered by the Roman legions, but by Caesar. It was not before the Carthaginian soldiers that Rome was made to tremble, but before Hannibal. It was not the Macedonian phalanx which penetrated to India, but Alexander. It was not the French Army which reached the Weser and the Inn, it was Turenne. Prussia was not defended for seven years against the three most formidable European powers by Prussian soldiers, but by Frederick the Great. It was Grant that defeated Lee, not the Federals.

J. F. C. Fuller
The Generalship of Ulysses S. Grant (p. 9–10)

An organization's personality *is* the leader's persona. To the list of legendary captains can rightly be added: It was not the valiant soldiers of the Confederacy who stood defiantly like a steel gray curtain between Grant and Richmond, but Lee. And it was not the gallant men in blue who drove Lee from the Rapidan to Appomattox, but *Grant*. To fully appreciate the meaning of great battles, we must understand the personalities of the generals who waged them and their ability to weld troops into living instruments of steel and resolve.

To fully understand highly competitive organizations, we must appreciate the personalities of the leaders who engineer their success; the leadership team's ability to galvanize employees through legitimate empowerment; and the leader's charismatic influence on the whole organization.

COMMON SENSE

[Grant's] success was sheer common sense . . .

Gen. Joseph Johnston
Leading American Soldiers (p. 137)

Quite uneducated in military matters, he relied entirely on his personality and his common sense, intuitively understanding that war is nothing more than an equation between pressure and resistance; that all direction springs from these two, and if the direction of an operation is to be profitable its object must be a desirable one, and its objective, or goal, an attainable one with the means at hand. Grant's common sense is so remarkable, that in itself it constitutes a military lesson of no small importance, namely, that the art of war—strategy and tactics—is nothing more than action adapted to circumstances.

J. F. C. Fuller
The Generalship of Ulysses S. Grant (p. 185)

Evil-minded people were trying to make our men believe that Grant and Lincoln were making this long delay in front of Petersburg in order to secure their continuance in office. But this was an outrage upon those noble characters, and an insult to the common sense of every man among us. We knew that the surest way for our high officials to hold their place was by no means to court delay, but to strike a quick, bold blow at the enemy.

Joshua Chamberlain
The Passing of the Armies (p. 25)

Common sense is judgment without analysis. To refer to the words *common sense* contradicts them. Most leaders don't use *common* sense at all. Common sense is really *uncommon* sense.

26

COMPETITOR ANALYSIS

My experience in the Mexican war was to great advantage to me afterwards. Besides the many practical lessons it taught, the war brought nearly all the officers of the regular army together so as to make them personally acquainted. It also brought them in contact with volunteers, many of whom served in the war of the rebellion afterwards.

The acquaintance thus formed was of immense service to me in the war of the rebellion—I mean what I learned of the characters of those to whom I was afterwards opposed. I do not pretend to say that all movements, or even many of them, were made with special reference to the characteristics of the commander against whom they were directed. But my appreciation of my enemies was certainly affected by this knowledge. The natural disposition of most people is to clothe a commander of a large army whom they do not know, with almost superhuman abilities. A large part of the National army, for instance, and most of the press of the country, clothed General Lee with just such qualities, but I had known him personally, and knew that he was mortal; and it was just as well that I felt this.

U. S. Grant
The Personal Memoirs of Ulysses S. Grant (p. 115–16)

Urging caution, he . . . uncharacteristically proceeded slowly. He was beginning to get a feel for the wiles of his enemy, and was afraid Lee had an unpleasant surprise for him. Indeed, when Grant discovered how Lee was welcoming him to North Anna, he ground to a halt. Lee had devised V-shaped earthworks.

Anderson and Anderson
The Generals (p. 395)

No competitor is as dangerous as an uncommitted employee. The enemy may be at home. One's chief competitor is oneself. The marketplace is an economic battlefield set aside where organizations may play at deceiving and out-competing each other. The principal difference in a civil war and business competitiveness is this: a civil war is like the heat of the fever, and a business competition is like the heat of exercise. After all, an organization is a collection of business people of recognizable cohesion, held together by a common competitor. To paraphrase an old Mongolian proverb—a competitor's greatest work is to break his enemies, drive them out of their fortifications, take from them all their customers, hear the silence of their technologies and the weeping of their leaders, and welcome the smiles of their customers.

COMPLIANCE

It was very doubtful whether Congress would declare war; but if Mexico should attack our troops, the Executive could announce, "Whereas, war exists by the acts of, etc." and prosecute the contest with vigor. Once initiated there were but few public men who would have the courage to oppose it. Experience proves that the man who obstructs a war in which his nation is engaged, no matter whether right or wrong, occupies no enviable place in life or history. Better for him, individually, to advocate "war, pestilence, and famine," than to act as obstructionist to a war already begun.

U. S. Grant in William S. McFeely's
Grant: A Biography (p. 30)

Compliance vaporizes force. Joining a parade already in progress is intelligent compliance. Organizations going through change hesitate at everything and support everyone. Leaders entering organizations with change in process will learn more by merging with the mainstream for a while, instead of contradicting direction or forcing extremes.

CONSENSUS

I believe it is better for a commander charged with the responsibility of all the operations of his army to consult his generals freely but informally, and get their views and opinions, and then make up his mind what action to take and act accordingly. There is too much truth in the old adage, "Councils of war do not fight."

U. S. Grant in Horace Porter's
Campaigning with General Grant (p. 226)

Grant kept his own counsel, almost to the extent of stolidity.

Joshua Chamberlain
The Passing of the Armies (p. 381)

When leaders yield, there is no resistance; when leaders insist, there is no yielding. Consensual validation of points of view held by a leader's direct reports during planning and problem-solving sessions produce synergistic outcomes. Consensus seeking offers the promise of marshaling the team's resources to achieve agreed-upon outcomes without denying anyone's worth. The best results flow from a fusion of creativity, logic, insight, information, and emotion. Increased buy-in is a result of discussion. When the team's power is focused, a critical mass develops. Some leaders make the mistake of using consensus as a decision-making tool instead of recognizing it as a barometer of commitment. It is important to strive for consensus, but the critical mass of ownership for effective implementation should be the goal. Total buy-in is nice, but not necessary to achieve overall success.

CONSEQUENCES

Nations, like individuals, are punished for their transgressions.

U. S. Grant
The Personal Memoirs of
Ulysses S. Grant (p. 38)

Consequences elevated to contingencies become repercussion management. As leaders of organizations or teams, what you do and say always has consequences and for every action there is a reaction. Good decisions usually bring positive results. Poor decisions and attitudes generally produce negative outcomes. See consequences as calisthenics for change.

CONTINUOUS IMPROVEMENT

Grant believed that, in war, what is won is only a fulcrum on which to rest the lever for another effort. . . . He was always ready to move against his enemy: he was never petrified by numbers or situations, and never through fear or caution did he exaggerate the strength of his enemy . . .

Adam Badeau
Military History of Ulysses S. Grant, Vol. 1 (p. 127)

His tactics are simplicity itself—the forward thrust, under cover of which each successive flanking movement is made; but failure to understand the true use of artillery, and the great difficulty of using this arm in wooded country, threw the onus of his numerous holding attacks on to his infantry, who, consequently, suffered heavy casualties. Battling with earthworks, rivers, swamps, and men, here again we find another heroic soul; accepting all consequences, never being obsessed by misfortune, fearing no danger, bearing up against disappointments, Grant strode onwards from battlefield to battlefield, fashioning each loss into a stepping-stone towards the next hoped-for success.

J. F. C. Fuller
The Generalship of Ulysses S. Grant (p. 380)

[Porter] recalls a very pertinent criticism [of Grant] made . . . by General Sherman. He said: "Grant always seemed pretty certain to win when he went into a fight with anything like equal numbers. I believe the chief reason why he was more successful than others was that while they were thinking so much about what the enemy was going to do, Grant was thinking all the time about what he was going to do himself."

Horace Porter
Campaigning with General Grant (p. 65)

Eternal vigilance is the price leaders pay for continuous improvement. Each quality improvement becomes a "fulcrum on which to rest the lever for another effort." The old maxim *success breeds success* is one of the guiding principles of a continuous improvement effort. Each block of improvement builds on the foundation of methodical, planned change. Once the improvement machinery swings into full gear, the step-by-calculated-step efforts produce immediate rewards and visible improvement.

Paying attention helps people see patterns and uncover relationships between work processes. Deliberate attempts to hunt for improvements produce results. Continuous improvement turns out to be *gap* management or *iota* management. Gaps between what is and what is wanted create dissonance. Dissonance creates awareness for change. This increased awareness creates an attitude to manage the change process one improvement (iota) at a time to keep change manageable and positive.

COOL RESOLVE

One soldier who had been fighting on the hill watched Grant stand "cool and calculating" with a cigar in his mouth ordering fresh assaults over bloody ground. When things [went] poorly, he acted as if that was exactly how he expected them to go, and sent new men in to make them go better.

William S. McFeely
Grant: A Biography (p. 131)

Grant rode over to see Wallace just before the attack began. He looked fresh and unworried, and when he said "Good morning" he did not sound like a man who had been within inches of a disastrous defeat twelve hours earlier; looking back long afterward, Wallace put into words a thought that struck many men, at various times: "If he had studied to be undramatic, he could not have succeeded better."

William S. McFeely
Grant: A Biography (p. 131)

Cool, dispassionate resolve is indefatigable determination. Such coolness drives outcomes that are hard to obtain without glacial perseverance. Sometimes leaders, like Grant, have to detach themselves from the murderous, filthy work at hand to remain objective enough to lead. Any manager who has been involved in reorganizations, downsizings, mergers, and buyouts knows exactly what Grant was going through as he stood "cool and calculating . . . ordering fresh assaults over bloody ground."

COURAGE

───∞∽───

... Grant was no ordinary general; for he was one of those rare and
strange men who are fortified by disaster in place of being depressed.

J. F. C. Fuller
Grant and Lee (p. 147)

Courage is violated by cowardice and outraged by silence. These
are yeasty times. Inexorable change moves steadily across organizational landscapes, sometimes creeping, other times vaulting over
organizations unwilling or unable to get out of the way. Some leaders
succumb to the relentless pressure of change, whereas others, like
Grant, are no "ordinary" leaders. They are people who are "fortified
by disaster in place of being depressed."

Courage is a word not used enough in management circles. Tom
Peters, leadership consultant and co-author of *Passion for Excellence,*
uses it: "Coaching, teaching and transmitting values, more than any
other responsibility, demand dramatic skills. It is vital that the show
you put on not be fraudulent in any way . . . your people will judge
your integrity."[3]

It takes considerable courage to lead any organization through these
turbulent, chaotic, competitive waters. Oftentimes leaders find themselves up creeks without paddles. Leadership is a lonely business at
the top. It will take all the courage leaders can muster in the days
ahead. Such bravery in trials and tribulations, though, is an American
tradition—one that is outraged by silence and violated by cowardice.

CRITICS

My . . . experience has taught me two lessons: first, that things are seen plainer after the events have occurred; second, that the most confident critics are generally those who know the least about the matter criticized.

U. S. Grant
The Personal Memoirs of Ulysses S. Grant (p. 100)

That the [newspaper's] criticism stung Grant painfully is obvious. Not long after the battle he did something which he did rarely, if ever, at any other time in his military career: he wrote a letter to an editor in reply to newspaper criticism.

Bruce Catton
Grant Moves South (p. 256–57)

One victory scatters a hundred critics. Even a partial success silences some critics. Grant usually interrupted obnoxious critics by giving them victories.

CROSS-FUNCTIONAL TEAMS

In the battle of Chattanooga, troops from the Army of the Potomac, from the Army of the Tennessee, and from the Army of the Cumberland participated. In fact, the accidents growing out of the heavy rains and the sudden rise in the Tennessee River so mingled the troops that the organizations were not kept together, under their respective commanders, during the battle.

Indeed, I doubt whether officers or men took any note at the time of the fact of this intermingling of commands. All saw a defiant foe surrounding them, and took it for granted that every move was intended to dislodge him, and it made no difference where the troops came from so that the end was accomplished.

U. S. Grant
The Personal Memoirs of
Ulysses S. Grant (p. 387)

Does the mortar between the stones in a wall hold the stones together or keep them apart? As teams begin, they conclude. As they evolve, they confront. As they understand, they act as one. Superior cross-functional teams act out of group inquiry, more than sectional advocacy. When the parts consider themselves greater than the whole, seamless relationships across departments are impossible. For organizations to be successful in today's economy, they must manage the space between cross-functional areas. Divisional drawbridges must be lowered. High-turfed kingdoms and fiefdoms must allow passport-free travel. Do the boundaries or communication, or policies, or vested interest between departments in an organization hold the organization together or . . . ?

CUMULATIVE COMPETENCE

Grant is a wonderful example of this: of how a man of forty could begin with a Belmont and end with an Appomattox campaign. He was forever learning, and though not endowed with outstanding genius, through sheer industry, perseverance, and self-education he accomplished his end far more thoroughly than many a more brilliant but less determined general would have done.

J. F. C. Fuller
The Generalship of Ulysses S. Grant (p. 8)

The fact is, troops who have fought a few battles and won, and followed up their victories, improve upon what they were before to an extent that can hardly be counted by percentage. The difference in result is often decisive victory instead of inglorious defeat.

U. S. Grant
*The Personal Memoirs
of Ulysses S. Grant* (p. 400)

Grant was developing as a military realist. The war had taught him a few good lessons: that when untrained armies face each other, neither general gains by deferring a fight until the training of his own men is perfected; that in any hard battle there comes a time when both armies are ready to quit, and that the one which can nerve itself for one more attack at such a time is very likely to win; that troop morale is better in an active campaign than in training camp; that war means fighting, so that feints and demonstrations accomplish little, and the real object of a campaign is not to make the enemy retreat but to destroy him root and branch.

Bruce Catton
Grant Moves South (p. 217)

Yet something important was occurring with Grant himself. He was learning his trade. His experience as regimental quartermaster in the Mexican War had taught him a great deal about the way supplies are kept moving to an army in the field; here in Cairo he was getting a postgraduate course in this, discovering that all of the quartermasters' arrangements will break down unless the man at the top makes it his business to keep the cumbersome machinery moving.

Bruce Catton
Grant Moves South (p. 61)

The absence of cumulative competence *is* the learning disability of leaders and organizations. Learning is an accumulation of experience that causes a fundamental shift in consciousness, thinking, and feeling. The problem with the word "learning" is that most people, leaders included, lose sight of its real meaning, which is *meta* (above or beyond) and *noia* (mind). Learning has become synonymous with "taking in" information (like a sponge). Instead, it is the interplay between what is sensually experienced; when and where learning takes place; and how the individual reacts to, translates, and transforms the information received.

Real learning is a process and involves four dynamic phases, indelicately referred to as: unconscious incompetence, conscious incompetence, conscious competence, and unconscious competence. Unconscious incompetence means that the learner does not recognize inefficiency or ignorance in a certain area or skill. Conscious incompetence is the awareness of a need for improvement and a conscious recognition that the skill or knowledge is incomplete in a particular area. Conscious competence means that the learner is constantly aware of and pays particular attention to the imperfect progress in the area through skill practice.

Unconscious competence occurs when the skill is practiced and perfected to the point that it becomes second nature, and occurs unconsciously yet consummately in a given area of expertise.

DECENCY

Riding back to headquarters in the twilight, Grant passed many dead and wounded men from both armies. One scene particularly struck him: A Federal lieutenant and a Confederate private, both desperately wounded, lay side by side, and the lieutenant was trying without much success to give the Confederate a drink from his canteen. Grant reined in and looked at the two, then asked his staff officers if anyone had a flask. One officer finally produced one; Grant took it, dismounted, and walked to the two wounded men, giving each man a swallow of brandy. The Confederate murmured, "Thank you, General," and the Federal, too weak to speak, managed to flutter one hand in an attempt at a salute. Grant called to Rawlins: "Send for stretchers; send for stretchers at once for these men." As the stretcher party came up Grant got on his horse, then he noticed that the stretcher bearers, picking up the Union Officer, seemed inclined to ignore the Confederate.

"Take this Confederate, too," he ordered. "Take them both together; the war is over between them."

The men were borne away, and Grant and his party rode off.

Bruce Catton
Grant Moves South (p. 173)

Ord's troops had a hard march, groping along a narrow road in a swamp, where heavy bushes and a tangle of decayed logs constricted all movement. They remembered, once, how Grant tried to ride past the marching column, found that his horse was spattering the soldiers with mud, and left the road to pick his way through the underbrush, not returning to the road until he had reached the head of the column. An Ohio private recalled that the men were ready to cheer him for his considerate act, and wrote that the little incident "shows the kind of man on whose shoulders the greatest responsibilities were to be placed.

Charles W. Wright
A Corporal's Story: Experiences in the Ranks
of Company C, 81st Ohio Volunteer Infantry (p. 54)

Decency is status elevating kindness. The thin veil of decency is all that separates most organizations, however impressive, from the tyranny of excessive force and exploitation that lie dormant beneath the surface. Make no mistake about it: such tyranny is possible since organizations are microcosms of society. It takes decent and ethical leadership at the top to "send for stretchers" and "pick [the] way through the underbrush" to show people how highly you regard them. Grant treated his men as equals. Dr. Martin Luther King, Jr. would have applauded Grant's moves: "I have a dream that one day this nation will rise up and live out the true meaning of this creed—We hold these truths to be self-evident: that all men are created equal . . . "[4] No amount of rhetoric can replace an act of simple decency bestowed by a leader on a subordinate.

DECISION MAKING

The speed with which he roared through bureaucratic details prompted an officer to ask Grant if he was sure he was always right. "No," Grant answered, "I am not, but in war anything is better than indecision. *We must decide.* If I am wrong we shall soon find it out and can do the other thing. But *not to decide* wastes both time and money and may ruin everything." Grant as a coy political candidate was equally novel.

Anderson and Anderson
The Generals (p. 353)

The semantics of decision making demands choosing, not choice. The difference between making a decision and deciding is considerable. Grant recognized it. Deciding is looking for what is right. A decision is acting, hoping the choice is right. "Not to decide" as Grant warned "wastes both time and money and may ruin everything." Having one answer does not require a decision, only compliance—and maybe guts. Having many answers demands a decision-making process to get the right answer.

There are really just two outcomes to any decision-making process; either you alter the outcomes or you alter yourself. When you cannot eliminate problems, you must manage them instead of allowing them to manage you. Until leaders can integrate into one analytical process the semantics of decision making, particularly its impact on people, there can be no discipline, no science of management.

DEFINING MOMENTS

~~~

. . . [Grant] could not get back to Galena just now, and he did an odd thing; he discarded his colonel's uniform, even though he had not yet paid off the debt he had run up in order to buy it, and now he wore whatever clothing came to hand, with no insignia of rank. Did the promotion mark such a turning point in his own inner life that he would wear no uniform at all until he could don the one that belonged with the new commission?

William C. Church
*Ulysses S. Grant and the Period of National
Preservation and Reconstruction* (p. 84)

Nevertheless, those who had gone off to war with him could see in his success a glimmer of their own hopes. They were celebrating their own dreams when they cheered Grant—and gave him the presidency . . . Once he had become general, he had to go on to be president, and once his time was up, he had, again, no idea what to do with himself. But the difference was that he had heard those cheers and he could not do without them.

William S. McFeely
Grant: A Biography (p. xiii)

Defining moments are shouts of defiance against mediocrity. Crucibles of experience can serve as pivotal events, and become defining moments in a leader's—and an organization's—life. Such turning points totally destroy the mediocrity of what was and forge, instantaneously, the new person—the next generation of an organization.

DELAY

If you delay attack any longer the mortifying spectacle will be witnessed of a rebel army moving for the Ohio River . . . Let there be no further delay. Delay no longer for weather or reinforcements.

U. S. Grant in a letter to one of his generals
The Personal Memoirs of Ulysses S. Grant (p. 568)

One of the most anxious periods of my experience during the rebellion was the last few weeks before Petersburg. I felt that the situation of the Confederate army was such that they would try to make an escape at the earliest practicable moment, and I was afraid, every morning, that I would awake from my sleep to hear that Lee had gone, and that nothing was left but a picket line. He had his railroad by the way of Danville south, and I was afraid that he was running off his men and all stores and ordnance except such as it would be necessary to carry with him for his immediate defense. I knew he could move much more lightly and more rapidly than I, and that, if he got the start, he would leave me behind so that we would have the same army to fight again farther south—and the war might be prolonged another year.

U. S. Grant
The Personal Memoirs of Ulysses S. Grant (p. 592)

Missed opportunities create vacuums in performance. Manage well the thousands of impressionable moments in which people, customers, and organizations come into contact with you. Response-ability, particularly an organization's recovery skill, is the litmus test of the effectiveness of any service system, product development cycle, or personal relationship.

DELEGATION

When the word came that his troops were exchanging fire with rebels [in the Wilderness campaign] Grant sat down on the ground with his back against a small pine, picked up a piece of wood and started whittling.

Gene Smith
Lee and Grant (p. 190)

When I arrived I went to Sherman's headquarters, and we were at once closeted together. I showed him the instructions and orders under which I visited him. I told him that I wanted him to notify General Johnston that the terms which they had conditionally agreed upon had not been approved in Washington, and that he was authorized to offer the same terms I had given General Lee. I sent Sherman to do this himself. I did not wish the knowledge of my presence to be known to the army generally; so I left it to Sherman to negotiate the terms of the surrender solely by himself, and without the enemy knowing that I was anywhere near the field. As soon as possible I started to get away, to leave Sherman quite free and untrammeled.

U. S. Grant
The Personal Memoirs of Ulysses S. Grant (p. 645)

Delegation is not abdicating responsibility; it is escalating it exponentially. People feel empowered when a climate exists that provides them with the resources, skills, knowledge, information, and authority to take action. Leaders who move empowerment rhetoric to action grant more practical autonomy by whittling away at obstacles that block sustained and healthy performance. Theodore Roosevelt would probably have whittled alongside of Grant: "The best executive is the one who has sense enough to pick good men to do what he wants done, and self-restraint enough to keep from meddling with them while they do it."[5]

Delegatory responsibilities work best when leaders know what to delegate to whom, when. A simple process might clarify the level and amount delegated to direct reports. Working from an instructional, learned competency perspective, leaders can delegate responsibilities along a continuum of competency. Starting from minimal ability to accept authority and responsibility to accepting full responsibility and accountability, the levels of delegation look something like this: Leader to direct report: Investigate the problem and give me the facts; let me know the alternatives, with pros and cons, then I'll decide; recommend a course of action for my approval; brief me then implement; take action, report what you did and what the results are; take action, communicate only if there are problems; take full responsibility, no need to communicate other than periodic reviews. The upshot of this is that leaders should assign tasks to the most junior manager who has the skills and rank to complete the assignment successfully. Of course, that means knowing your staff's strengths and weaknesses.

DERAILMENT

Lastly, turning to Grant, what do we see? Recrimination?—no; excuses?—no; blame?—no. His plan has been wrecked; victory has been bungled out of his hands; clouds are gathering in the Valley of Virginia: that he has failed is obvious, and he accepts failure not as a defeated man, but as one who sees in every failure a fresh incentive to further action. His reticence at this moment is truly heroic; it is work and not failure which absorbs him. Nothing unhinges him, or weakens his faith in himself and in final victory. He soars above his subordinates, forgetting their mistakes so that he may waste not a moment in shouldering aside their blunders and getting on with his task. If he cannot destroy Lee, then he will destroy his communications; if he cannot destroy his communications, then he will invest Petersburg. Though means vary, his idea remains constant; he holds fast to Lee, so that Sherman's maneuvers may continue.

J. F. C. Fuller
The Generalship of Ulysses S. Grant (p. 294–95)

Failures have been errors of judgment, not of intent.

U. S. Grant in William S. McFeely
Grant: A Biography (p. 442)

Ulysses Grant had a genius for survival.

William S. McFeely's
Grant: A Biography (p. 380)

Regard mistakes and misfires as learning laboratories. Experience never errs, only judgment. Crucifying yourself—or someone—for a mistake kills initiative and contributes to decision paranoia and learned helplessness. Analyze misfires, assess their impact, reload, and move on. Grant never allowed his troops to attack heavily entrenched fortifications head-on after his disastrous blunder at Cold Harbor. It was a marker event in his military career.

The pain associated with failure will be your most loyal and trustworthy ally.

DETERMINATION

Neither responsibility, nor turmoil, nor danger, nor pleasure, nor pain, impaired the force of [Grant's] resolution . . .

Gen. James B. Fry
Military Miscellanies (p. 295)

Lee's army will be your objective point. Wherever Lee goes, there you will go also.

U. S. Grant
The Personal Memoirs of Ulysses S. Grant (p. 416)

One of my superstitions had always been when I started to go anywhere, or to do anything, not to turn back, or stop until the thing intended was accomplished.

U. S. Grant
The Personal Memoirs of Ulysses S. Grant (p. 35)

I propose to fight it out on this line if it takes all summer.

U. S. Grant in Horace Porter's
Campaigning with General Grant (p. 187)

Determination is determined action. Successful leaders in any profession decide what they want to do, then spit on their hands to take a good grip. Determination is emotional movement forward in spite of intellectual doubts or physical incapacities along the rough competitive roads ahead. A man who appreciated Grant's determination to stick things out is Vince Lombardi, who says: "We know how rough the road will be, how heavy here the load will be, we know about the barricades that wait along the track, but we have set our soul ahead upon a certain goal ahead and nothing left from hell to sky shall ever turn us back."[6]

It is not quite giving up when giving in is okay. It is an absolute refusal to accept the staleness of mediocrity. Determination adds momentum to perseverance that strengthens resolve to force closure. It is always too soon to quit too soon.

DIPLOMATIC IMPUNITY

[Grant spelled out the terms of Lee's surrender in regards to disposition of the sidearms of the Confederate officers] . . . The officers to give their individual paroles not to take up arms against the Government of the United States until properly exchanged . . . The arms, artillery and public property to be stacked, and turned over . . . This will not embrace the sidearms of the officers, nor their private horses or baggage. This done, each officer and man will be allowed to return to their homes, not to be disturbed by United States authority so long as they observe their paroles . . .

U. S. Grant to R. E. Lee as
surrender terms at Appomattox in
The Personal Memoirs of Ulysses S. Grant (p. 631)

Grant's most sensitive touch was reserved for Lee himself. By suggesting that their respective officers might conduct the surrender, he was offering to spare the vanquished general the humiliation of appearing in person.

Anderson and Anderson
The Generals (p. 442)

Diplomacy is a political continuation of war. All leaders use diplomacy, but not all leaders are diplomatic. Grant was both at Appomattox. He knew that two of the most important *rules* in politics are: to keep poised and allow the opponent at least one way out. Grant also knew that he would have to live with his conscience long after he accepted Lee's surrender.

DIRECT REPORTS

As his relationship with Grant began, Meade, a devout patriot, offered to yield the command of the Army of the Potomac to Sherman if Grant needed the latter near at hand. Grant said no in words "complimentary" to Meade . . .

William S. McFeely
Grant: A Biography (p. 158)

Grant's . . . subordinates . . . felt that they would be left to the exercise of an intelligent judgment, that if they did their best, even if they did not succeed, they would never be made scapegoats; and if they gained victories they would be given the sole credit for whatever they accomplished.

Horace Porter
Campaigning with General Grant (p. 191)

The question of who devised the plan of march from Atlanta to Savannah is easily answered: *it was clearly Sherman, and to him also belongs the credit of its brilliant execution.*

U. S. Grant
The Personal Memoirs of Ulysses S. Grant (p. 562)

Appreciate your direct reports now and avoid the rush. Two types of direct reports respond well to compliments, consideration, and respect—men and women. Start a quiet campaign of writing thank-you notes or sending complimentary E-mail messages to deserving people. Taking time to personalize your appreciation will speak volumes. For example, in answer to "why was General MacArthur great?" Major General Courtney Whitney replied, "It was because he made his men feel that their contribution was an important one—that they were somebody."[7]

More than anything else, direct reports want authentic leadership. More than anything else leaders want genuine support. When the skills and commitment of leaders and direct reports are complementary, the entire organization benefits.

DISCIPLINE

Drill and discipline were worth more to our men than fortifications.

U. S. Grant
The Personal Memoirs of Ulysses S. Grant (p. 212)

Discipline is bridled liberty. Too often discipline has a negative connotation. It is usually associated with punishment, strictness, or limitation. Those are its means—the milestones within the *disciplining* process itself as it unfolds. Being disciplined has both its positive and negative aspects.

No amount of disciplining will hold someone prisoner in "fortifications" such as rules, policies, and procedures if that person sees the disciplining as punitive. Discipline must come through liberty. When it does, it is seen as a self-governing action, more on the self-denial and self-control side of the discipline process. Developing these kinds of self-imposed restraints is liberating, worth much more than hiding behind "fortifications."

EMPATHY

Ulysses Grant sat on the porch of Mr. McLean's red brick farm-house, deep in quiet thought. To the surprise and disgust of his staff, he had no desire to savor the capture of the army he could see camped on the hills to his right, behind the courthouse. . . . There was much cork-popping and laughter, but no plans for a victory trip to Richmond. Grant refused, saying he would not add to the distress of Virginians.

Anderson and Anderson
The Generals (p. 3, 6)

When news of the surrender first reached our lines our men commenced firing a salute of a hundred guns in honor of the victory. I at once sent word, however, to have it stopped. The Confederates were now our prisoners, and we did not want to exult over their downfall.

U. S. Grant
The Personal Memoirs of Ulysses S. Grant (p. 633)

If any Civil War soldier had a tough inner core, Grant was the man; but with it, in the early days, there was a sensitivity, a remembrance of past difficulties, that made him vulnerable.

Bruce Catton
Grant Moves South (p. 208)

The great leaders understand equity; others profit by inequities. Empathy is a continuation of self-healing through compassion. Sensitivity to another's pain is acknowledgement of one's own vulnerabilities. Attempts to reduce another's pain are the highest form of self-healing.

EMPOWERMENT

General Grant in his official report and subsequent histories, speaking of this repulse [from Five Forks to Dinwiddie], says: "Here General Sheridan displayed great generalship. Instead of retreating with his whole command on the main army, to tell the story of superior forces encountered, he deployed his cavalry on foot, leaving only mounted men enough to take charge of the horses. This compelled the enemy to deploy over a vast extent of wooded and broken country and made his progress slow."

This definition of great generalship was intended, no doubt, to reassure Sheridan; but it was encouraging all around. It would let quite a number of modest colonels, of both sides, into the temple of fame.

Joshua Chamberlain
The Passing of the Armies (p. 106)

Empowerment is not a staff infection. "People are empowered," says Cher Holton, Ph.D., "when a safe climate exists which provides them with the resources, skills, knowledge, information and authority to take action on areas directly related to their jobs."[8] Leaders can buy a direct report's time; they can purchase physical presence at a given place and time; they can even bargain for a measured number of skilled muscular movements per hour. But leaders cannot buy commitment or loyalty or love. Using words like participative management, total quality management, and empowerment won't do it either. What will do it is so simple most leaders fail to see it: take the labels off. The word "empowerment," like other labels, serializes what it attempts to describe. If you want empowerment, don't call it empowerment—just *do* the things mentioned above by Holton. Empowerment is not something you *do* to people; it's something you *get* in return for excellence in leadership.

EXPECTANCY

Ulysses S. Grant's entrance into Washington was the most successful in the history of American politics. It was done exactly right. He simply stopped by the White House, paid his call, and left everyone thinking it would be perfectly natural for him to move right in. He achieved his immediate goal of confirming his military authority, but as he did so he established a public personality that was unforgettable. Everyone had heard about him as a military hero. His picture was on patriotic posters; people had read of his battles and imagined him on battlefields in Tennessee and Mississippi. Now they saw him at the seat of the civilian government, and he looked just fine. He was consummately modest and quietly confident; the image held for the rest of his political career—and beyond, into history.

William S. McFeely
Grant: A Biography (p. 254)

Expectancy is anticipation at a higher pitch. Meanings to things are not found in situations, circumstances, or appearances, but in people. When people believe or begin to believe something is true (whether it is true or not), they create outcomes or consequences that actually make whatever is believed come true. Ulysses S. Grant's ascendency into the presidency is a classic example of the concept of expectancy or self-fulfilling prophecy of social psychology.

Leaders get the performance they expect. Subordinates will perform to the level of the leader's expectation. So expect brilliance. Demand the best. Inspire people to outperform themselves. Anticipate loyalty and passion for excellence. Predict efficiency and effectiveness. Favor decency and fair play.

EXPEDIENCY

[Grant] wrote nearly all his documents with his own hand, and seldom dictated to anyone even the most unimportant dispatch.

Horace Porter
Campaigning with General Grant (p. 7)

[Grant] seated himself on the ground at the foot of a tree, and was soon busy receiving dispatches and writing orders to officers conducting the advance.

Horace Porter
Campaigning with General Grant (p. 304)

Back-of-the-envelope calculations beat proposal churning or committee action any day. Spontaneous insights or instructions jotted down in the "heat of battle" serve as productivity spurs to action. Proposal-churning and bureaucratic rigmarole are built-in straitjackets which bridle, then suffocate, legitimate progress. Committee action and consensus building have their place in operational realities. However, using them as locomotives to drive performance in every case usually means slower movement toward defined objectives. Sometimes you've just got to sit down at the foot of a decision tree and dispatch immediate, intuitive judgments.

EXPONENTIAL ENCROACHMENT

I regarded it as humane to both sides to protect the persons of those found at their homes, but to consume everything that could be used to support or supply armies. Protection was still continued over such supplies as were within lines held by us and which we expected to continue to hold; but such supplies within the reach of Confederate armies. I regarded as much contraband as arms or ordnance stores. Their destruction was accomplished without bloodshed and rendered to the same result as the destruction of armies. I continued this policy to the close of the war. . . . This policy I believe exercised a material influence in hastening the end.

U. S. Grant
Memoirs of Ulysses S. Grant (p. 368–69)

Encroachment is the penetration strategy; muscle is the competitive reality. Grant knew two things about war. The Civil War was a modern war, and prosecution of such a war required an aggressive campaign against the labor force that was fighting him in the mills and factories as surely as soldiers faced him in the trenches. His war was against the Confederate States of America and not just its agents of war, its armies. Grant measured his military success by its economic and social implications as well.

Grant's encroachment strategy (market domination strategy) is valid today. Organizations attack markets in much the same way. They buy up smaller competitors in the target market, woo a competitor's top people away, enter into price wars, and blitz the market with advertising.

FACE VALUE

To Ulysses S. Grant an acquittal was an acquittal; innocence was innocence.

William S. McFeely
Grant: A Biography (p. 414)

He was honest . . . and literally, quite innocently, expected absolute honesty in return. For example: [Grant] trusted Halleck until he discovered that Halleck had undermined him during the war. One of his chief regrets during his presidency was that the people he trusted weren't worthy of his trust.

John Griffiths, U. S. Grant's great-
great-grandson, in a personal interview
with the author on July 29, 1994

An ounce of deception is worth a ton of manure. Grant erred in the only way a trusting man could. Great men trust until the trust is violated. Once violated, trust must be earned through verification. Once verified, trust is given again. If violated a second time, trust cannot be earned again because it has been spent.

FAMILY

The general's letters to his wife were very frequent during a campaign, and no pressure of official duties was ever permitted to interrupt this correspondence.

I found [Grant] in his shirt-sleeves engaged in a rough-and-tumble wrestling match with the two older boys. The lads had just tripped him up, and he was on his knees on the floor grappling with the youngsters, and joining in their merry laughter. I had several dispatches in my hand, and when he saw that I had come on business, he disentangled himself . . . rose to his feet . . . brushed the dust off his knees with his hands . . .

Horace Porter
Campaigning with General Grant (p. 37, 198)

She had always thought herself ugly, and she was embarrassed by her crossed eyes. [Julia] cringed at the attention of strangers because she felt they were staring at a spectacle, not admiring the wife of General Grant. When he left the celebration at St. Louis, Julia stayed behind. She said she had never before had "the courage to consent" to eye surgery, "but now that my husband had become so famous I really thought it behooved me to look as well as possible. So I consulted the doctor on this, to me; the most delicate subject, but alas! he told me it was too late, too late." Despondent, Julia timidly confessed to Grant that she had seen a doctor and nothing could be done. Grant responded by saying he liked her eyes "just as they are," and forbade her to "make any experiments, as I might not like you half so much with other eyes."

Anderson and Anderson
The Generals (p. 356)

My son accompanied me throughout the campaign and siege, and caused no anxiety either to me or to his mother, who was at home. He looked out for himself and was in every battle of the campaign. His age, then not quite thirteen, enabled him to take in all he saw, and to retain a recollection of it that would not be possible in more mature years.

U. S. Grant,
The Personal Memoirs of Ulysses S. Grant (p. 288)

At Quincy, Grant parted with his eleven-year-old son, Frederick Dent Grant, who had been with him ever since Grant became a colonel. Mrs. Grant and the children would be campaigners, in this war, and Grant would have some or all of them with him whenever he could. He sent Fred home now, supposing that Julia would be worried if he took the lad on into Missouri . . .

Bruce Catton
Grant Moves South, 1861–1876 (p. 11)

All leaders come from families. Make time for your family no matter how busy you are. Make time for your family no matter how busy you get. Make time for your family.

FOLLOW-THROUGH

As a result, each victory was followed by a long breathing spell. There was no real continuity to any program; a campaign would break up into isolated segments, and no advantage was ever followed up properly.

Bruce Catton from a suggestion
advanced by Maj. Gen. U. S. Grant III,
Grant Moves South (p. 280–81)

Follow-through is outcome management. Finishing up is taking the time for closure. It is seeing something through to a logical and, hopefully, profitable conclusion. Prosecuting *ends to things* tightens gaps that expose vulnerabilities or allow leakage.

FRIENDSHIP

Just before Halleck put an end to Grant's period of disgrace, there was a significant little ceremony in the ladies' cabin of the steamboat *Tigress,* which, anchored in the stream abreast of Fort Henry, was serving as Grant's headquarters boat. Surrounded by brigadiers and staff officers, Grant was called on to receive a presentation sword. The speech of presentation was made by Colonel C. C. Marsh, of the 20th Illinois, who remarked that the sword had been ordered a long time ago but that fortunately its delivery had been delayed.

The sword was handsome—ivory-handled and mounted in gold, as a newspaper correspondent saw it—and when he accepted it Grant choked up and was unable to stammer out a speech of thanks. He hurried out on deck, and Dr. Brinton found him there with tears in his eyes.

The presentation ceremony is worth dwelling on a moment. The sword was inscribed: Presented to Gen. U. S. Grant by G. W. Graham, C. R. Lagow, C. C. Marsh and Jno. Cook, and the date under these names was 1861: the Cairo period, when Grant was just setting up his military household, grappling to himself some, like Rawlins, who would do much good for him, and others who would do him harm. Captain Rowley, in the fall of 1862, would write to Washburn angrily denouncing four officers on Grant's staff, saying "I doubt if either of them have gone to bed sober for a week," and remarking that with such men around him it was small wonder if Grant occasionally kicked over the traces; and Lagow was one of the four Rowley named. Jno. Cook was the colonel whom the anonymous correspondent had blamed for the disappearance of captured food-stuffs at Fort Donelson, and G. W. Graham was the civilian who this correspondent had named. A former Cairo business man who had tied his fortunes to Grant's, Graham acted as headquarters sutler, kept a supply of cigars and liquor on hand.

Bruce Catton
Grant Moves South (p. 208–9)

Friends are profit, cliques are overhead. A leader has three faithful friends: a loyal executive secretary, voice mail, and cash flow.

FRONTLINE
MANAGEMENT

Company officers were either self-appointed, or elected by vote of the recruits, and in neither case was proper qualification for the job a factor. In time many of these became good officers—like the enlisted men, they were as smart as townfolks, and most of them were almost painfully conscientious—but in the beginning, almost without exception, they knew nothing about what they were supposed to do, and, by the time they had learned, a regiment almost inevitably developed certain defects that could never be cured. Any colonel who hoped to train and discipline his men had to start with the company officers, simply because it was their deficiencies that made discipline so lax and training so imperfect.

Bruce Catton
Grant Moves South, 1861–1863 (p. 8)

Be parochial in promoting people into frontline managerial positions. Why parochial? Because the frontline people you promote must know the work, its subtleties, its aggravations. They must know what excellence in their particular area looks like, feels like, tastes like. Select people who are top performers themselves and who also possess good people and communication skills.

As the management level closest to the work, frontline people are in the best position to supervise the work at hand. The chief mistake most leaders make is that they promote good technicians from the field into first-line supervisory positions without proper coaching and training. Most organizations do a poor job of succession planning at the supervisory level. Leaders who are serious about promoting and then developing operations managers must provide equitable compensation, recognition, and skills development. Make sure the frontline managers know they are the implementers, executors, liaisons between the "troops" and top management.

A fundamental leadership task is to ensure that frontline people are the heroes; that they are valued by top management. The role of everyone else (top management, staff, accounting, human resources) and everything else (rules, policies, technological resources) is to enhance line-supervision's ability to do the work. Success in today's frontline-dependent world will come when frontline managers and supervisors are honored as heroes and empowered to produce quality products and services.

Promote enthusiastic people who created excitement and zest among their colleagues and customers *before* they were considered for managerial positions. Reward people—with more responsibility and promotions—who take pride in their work and brag about the accomplishments of colleagues who elevate their level of performance. These kinds of people bring the workplace to a high pitch by generating a sense of purpose and urgency that compels colleagues to produce.

GOVERNMENT

No political party can or ought to exist when one of its corner-
stones is opposition to freedom of thought and to the right to worship
God according to the dictate of one's own conscience, or according to
the creed of any religious denomination whatever.

U. S. Grant
The Personal Memoirs of
Ulysses S. Grant (p. 127)

**Government's—any government's—chief job is to practice the
art of judicious hands-off.** This kind of "hands-off" philosophy
really works best. Leaders, whether government, private, or military,
would better serve their constituents by operating under the policy of
laissez-faire, laissez-passer. Leave it alone, and let it happen. In the
long run every governing body mirrors its people, the reflection being
wisdom and integrity or greed and stupidity. Anyone who leads would
be deepened—and humbled—by revisiting the great documents of
American history: The Declaration of Independence, The Constitution
of the United States of America, The Bill of Rights, Jefferson's First
Inaugural Address, The Emancipation Proclamation, Lincoln's Gettysburg Address, Kennedy's Inaugural Address.

Their messages are inspiring:

"We hold these truths to be self-evident, that all men are created
equal . . . "

"That to secure these rights, governments . . . [derive] their powers
from the consent of the governed . . . "

" . . . and that government of the people, by the people, for the people, shall not perish from the earth."

" . . . Ask not what your country can do for you, ask what you can
do for your country."[9]

GRANT'S HYDRAULIC
RELATIONSHIP TO LEE

In 1854, when Captain Ulysses S. Grant resigned from the army—a decision reputedly forced on him by his superiors because of habitual drunkenness, Lee was superintendent of the United States Military Academy at West Point. By 1860, when Grant had in six civilian years failed as a farmer, a real estate salesman, and was a clerk in his father's harness and leather-goods shop in Galena, Illinois, Colonel Robert E. Lee was commander of all United States Army forces in the Department of Texas. Scraping for a living, [Grant] wept on a street in Galena when no one bought a load of firewood he was peddling.

Charles Bracelen Flood
Lee: The Last Years (p. 7)

Yesterday's accomplishments are today's prerequisites. When preparation meets opportunity, the relevance—or irrelevance—of the preparation becomes obvious. The quality of the preparation magnetizes experiences that polish its rough edges or smooth its refinements. Grant needed polishing; Lee needed refining. The country needed them both.

GUTS

At the height of the celebration loaded steamers were seen coming from the Columbus side of the river. The rebel troops driven from the camp had re-formed and were coming back. Suddenly a Federal disaster seemed in the making. "We are surrounded and will have to surrender!" an officer cried.

"I guess not," Grant replied. "If we are surrounded we must cut our way out just as we cut our way in." Under his leadership the troops fell back toward their boats. Bullets sang around them, and at one point a confederate detachment came within 50 feet of where Grant was. He looked at them a moment and then turned his borrowed horse and walked the animal away slowly. Only when he was out of their sight did he put the horse into a gallop. At the landings he waited until everyone else was aboard the boats, then turned from the advancing rebels and put his horse down the steep riverbank onto a single gangplank resting on the ships rail, and from there, with a bound, down onto the deck. It was nicely done. His men raised a cheer. His doggedness, calm, tranquility, a Wellington-like steadiness, had saved the day. The men knew it.

Gene Smith
Lee and Grant (p. 111)

Leading from behind is an oxymoron. Leading people through technological skirmishes, economic battlefields, and competitive wars is not for the faint of heart. Leading takes guts. It demands fearlessness as a rule and gallantry as policy.

Heroic acts are tempting but not necessarily resigning to death's premature embrace. They are monuments of courage, conscious acts of heroic intentionality to master one's fate.

Grant's courage and gut-wrenching resolve are well known. Even in the most trying circumstances, "doggedness, calm, tranquility, a Wellington-like steadiness . . . saved the day." People who have any thought of accepting, or keeping, the mantle of leadership will have to back up rhetoric with daring most of the time and raw guts some of the time.

HARMONIC CONVERGENCE

Below the fort something more important than anyone present could understand was taking place: an army was coming into existence. What Grant had with him was, up to this moment, simply a collection of individual regiments. Never before had all of them been brought together in one place. The habit of co-ordination had not been born; these regiments had been enlisted, organized, and drilled separately, and they had seen so little of the parade ground that, as one veteran remarked afterward, they were to get their baptism of fire "before they learned that the cardinal military sin was to guide left while passing in review." They had been inadequately drilled, what their commanders knew about handling massed troops was something that would have to be learned on the battlefield . . .

Bruce Catton
Grant Moves South (p. 142)

Develop teams not facsimiles. All of the best organizations, every revolutionary advance in technology, each element in heightened service distinction is team built. Teams work when leadership works. Grant was working to create, enhance the skills of his troops, and build synergy, although he didn't call it that. But his army, his team, was "coming into existence." When the *whole* coordinates efforts and achieves greater results than one part (individuals, units, committees) the result is a harmonic convergence of talents, mission, and resources.

However, harmony, synergy, and coordination, once achieved, are ephemeral qualities in even the best teams. The reality of team leadership is that team excellence needs leaders who care. Those who are interested enough to dismantle barriers to performance, respectful enough to listen nonjudgmentally, trusting enough to allow innovation, and fair enough to match rewards with performance.

HAZARDOUS DUTY

His sense of urgency reflected a judgment that if the Confederacy was not subdued in the first months of 1862, it would be far more difficult to defeat later. He knew that battles would have to be fought, and friends killed. Other generals could not face such facts; their hesitation about subjecting themselves, their friends, and the men under their command to the hazards of battle is deplored—by experts—as vacillation. Cold-eyed men who can accept the proposition that postponed battles may kill more men than immediate ones consider a hesitating general's sense of humanity in the midst of a war to be misplaced. They think little of reluctant generals, perhaps learned in tactics but unprepared for carnage, who balk at the realities of war. They admire, instead, Ulysses S. Grant's simple logic, which he worked with such messy terror at Shiloh.

William S. McFeely
Grant: A Biography (p. 110)

Hazardous duty is still duty. Avoiding hazards is no safer in the long run than outright exposure. Grant knew that from personal experience—"postponed battles may kill more men [eventually] than immediate ones." Grant knew the country was severely wounded. As a product of frontier life, he knew with absolute certainty that when something is mortally wounded the humane thing to do is to put the wounded *thing* (animal, plant, or bruised ego) out of its misery. Heal or bury the animal. Prune or compost the plant. Praise or provide therapy for the bruised ego. As for an ailing country, he knew he must put the rebellion to rest.

HIRING THE RIGHT STUFF

Do not hesitate to give commands to officers in whom you have confidence, without regard to claims of others on account of rank. What we want is prompt and active movements . . .

> U. S. Grant in Horace Porter's
> *Campaigning with General Grant* (p. 190)

It is men who wait to be selected, and not those who seek, from whom we may always expect the most efficient service.

> U. S. Grant
> *The Personal Memoirs of Ulysses S. Grant* (p. 405)

Everyone knew why he was in town; Grant was to be a lieutenant general . . . Lincoln went over to him: "Why, here is General Grant! Well, this is a great pleasure." They shook hands warmly. Then the president chatted in a friendly way. Grant pulled at his lapel and lowered his head shyly; but his eyes met Lincoln's. The two men were off to exactly the right start.

> William S. McFeely
> *Grant: A Biography* (p. 154)

Promote the right people and fire the wrong attitudes. The ultimate testimony to your worth is not so much what you get out of leadership, but what you bring to it. Competence in your leadership role prepares you for greater responsibility. Those who covet the next promotional opportunity usually miss relevant—and defining—work experience. Fast-trackers eventually suffer from *competence anorexia* on their rocket ride to the top of organizational charts. Competence building simply means time-in-grade. Acceleration has more to do with timing. Let circumstance ask the question and job performance answer the challenge.

HOLE MANAGEMENT

Grant had experienced a change of mind—a complete and decided one. His imperative order now received meant giving up entirely the position we had just been ordered to entrench, across the hard-won White Oak Road.

Joshua Chamberlain
The Passing of the Armies (p. 93)

Grant followed the first rule of "hole management": When you find yourself in one, stop digging! Holes, potholes, pits, craters, and abysses are all places leaders do not want to be. Key stakeholders in the leader's as well as the organization's success would agree. The best kind of hole management is to stay out of one. When you find yourself throwing money down one—stop! If you intend to hold onto an old technology—don't! If customer service is falling through some cracks—plug 'em up! If your people's skills are becoming obsolete—train them, quickly! Never settle for a low return on investment.

HOSTILE TAKEOVERS

The people who had been in rebellion must necessarily come back into the Union, and be incorporated as an integral part of the nation. Naturally the nearer they were placed to an equality with the people who had not rebelled, the more reconciled they would feel with their old antagonists, and the better citizens they would be from the beginning. They surely would not make good citizens if they felt that they had a yoke around their necks.

U. S. Grant
The Personal Memoirs of Ulysses S. Grant (p. 642)

Takeovers are bludgeoning devises. If leaders want to study the social, economic, and political implications and fallout of mergers, reorganizations, downsizing, and hostile takeovers—study hell.

THE HUMAN SIDE
OF WAR

As we would look around the corner we could see the streets and the Appomattox bottom, presumably near the bridge, packed with the Confederate army. I did not have artillery brought up, because I was sure Lee was trying to make his escape, and I wanted to push immediately in pursuit. At all events I had not the heart to turn the artillery upon such a mass of defeated and fleeing men, and I hoped to capture them soon.

U. S. Grant, a day
before Lee's surrender.
The Personal Memoirs of Ulysses S. Grant (p. 609)

Simple actions reflect intense commitment. Grant knew that it was ridiculous to bludgeon people into submission. He knew the difference between power and force. He obviously recognized that people were flesh and blood. They were not a bundle of movable assets to be discarded or destroyed.

Make no mistake about it, leaders who cultivate a sensitivity toward personal dignity and worth, instill a sense of fair play and hope, and demand genuine commitment at all levels will enjoy phenomenal success.

ICY INSIGHT

The most important part of [Grant's growing] knowledge was something he carried with him as an almost private joke. He had learned—or had somehow always known—how simple war is. It may have dawned on him as he dozed while sitting erectly at a lecture at West Point, or during the more intense seminar of a Mexican War battle, or at almost any other time. When he learned the lesson does not matter. He knew it. The truth underlying it was uncongenial to American ears, and Grant was too kind and gentle a man ever to come out with it directly. But his whole life was focused on his mastery of the fact and his *Memoirs* was its record: war is an act; to make war is to kill.

William S. McFeely
Grant: A Biography (p. 78)

Leaders can work in the shadow of an important insight without grasping it. Grant was pressed by hardship and pushed by circumstance all of his life. He understood the weight of adversity, the callousness of suffering, the heartlessness of misfortune, the gravity of pain, the punishment of poverty. He understood because hardships were his constant companions. He experienced their viselike grip. He recognized their tandem nature.

It was cold, painful experience that gave Grant the insight that "war is an act; to make war is to kill." His icy detachment was the product of the furnace of experience, not emotional numbness. Leaders must recognize that when organizations compete for market share, they are at war with competitors. Those who dominate markets win. Those who don't, scramble or die. Those who are well niched thrive. The rest adapt or die. There *is* a certain ruthlessness to enterprise. To win markets is to kill or cripple or outmaneuver the competition.

IMPLEMENTATION

The confederacy was providing Union strategists with abundant proof that conquests made on the map mean nothing as long as enemy armies themselves are undefeated.

Bruce Catton
Grant Moves South (p. 307)

If you fail to implement, you are constipating the plan. Unbiased (hopefully) data collection, hypothesis generation, rigorous analytical reasoning, and comprehensive testing are all necessary ingredients in forming a plan of action. Leaders must link strategy with action or the strategy turns out to be inaction. Inept planning is paralysis by analysis. Inept implementation is paralysis by passivity.

IMPRESSION MANAGEMENT

Years afterward, Dana tried to sum up his impression of Grant; and his words are obviously the words of a man who has rubbed elbows with someone profoundly out of the ordinary, but who cannot quite say just how or why he was so impressed.

Grant was an uncommon fellow—the most modest, the most disinterested and the most honest man I ever knew, with a temper that nothing could disturb and a judgment that was judicial in its comprehensiveness and wisdom. Not a great man except morally; not an original or brilliant man, but sincere, thoughtful, deep and gifted with courage that never faltered; when the time came to risk all, he went in like a simple-hearted, unaffected, unpretending hero, whom no ill omens could deject and no triumph unduly exalt. A social, friendly man, too, fond of a pleasant joke and also ready with one, but liking above all a long chat of an evening, and ready to sit up all night talking in the cool breeze in front of his tent. Not a man of sentimentality, not demonstrative in friendship, but always holding to his friends and just even to the enemies he hated.

William W. Thayer
From Tannery to the White House:
The Life of Ulysses S. Grant (p. 6)

Other men were coming to the same sort of conclusion. Even the New York World, which had attacked Grant so bitterly a little earlier, was beginning to see him in a different light. Its correspondent wrote, almost as if he were saying it against his will:

"General Grant still retains his hold upon the affections of his men. His energy and disposition to do something is what they admire in him and he had the remarkable tact of never spoiling any mysterious and vague notions which may be entertained in the minds of the privates as to the qualities of a commander-in-chief. He confines himself to saying and doing as little as possible before his men."

"No Napoleonic displays, no ostentation, no speech, no superfluous flummery. Thus distance lends enchantment to the view of the man. The soldiers observe him coming and rising to their feet gather on each side of the way to see him pass—they do not salute him, they only watch him . . . with a certain sort of familiar reverence. His abstract air is not so great while he thus moves along as to prevent his seeing everything without apparently looking at it; you will see this in the fact that however dense the crowd in which you stand, if you are an acquaintance his eye will for an instant rest on yours with a glance of recollection and with it a grave nod of recognition. A plain blue suit, without scarf, sword or trappings of any sort, save the double-starred shoulder straps—an indifferently good beard of a cross between 'light' and 'sandy'; a square-cut face whose lines and contour indicate extreme endurance and determination, complete the external appearance of this small man, as one sees him passing along, turning and chewing restless the end of his unlighted cigar."

A quote from *New York Herald* article
in William S. McFeely's
Grant: A Biography (p. 39)

Grant held Lee in an iron vise, whose tightening was such that the impression was always present that he possessed a reserve of force not yet brought into play. So in the end it was futile to oppose him. He always had something left—always kept something back . . . The suggestion of power held back.

Gene Smith
Lee and Grant (p. 236)

Managing impressions is managing results. Most leaders underestimate the importance of a good professional image. If there is one impression management challenge leaders share, it is the consistent ability to make good impressions. Regardless of the methods used, the art of generating commitment in others is, to a great degree, dependent on the personality of the leader. Charismatic leaders seem to draw people magically to their side. They have the uncanny ability to touch the hearts and the minds of their people.

Believe it or not, Ulysses S. Grant had a charismatic influence over his men—over the entire Federal forces, for that matter. Although he displayed "no Napoleonic [behavior], no ostentation, no speech, no superfluous flummery," Grant was idolized as a leader who "retains his hold upon the affections of his men." The message for leaders of any era: People *want* to carry out the plans of the charismatic leader— often without even being asked or prodded.

IN-BASKET MANAGEMENT

The difficulty is in finding commanding officers possessed of suffi-
cient breadth of view and administrative ability to confine their attention to perfecting their organizations, and giving a general supervision
to their commands, instead of wasting their time upon details.

U. S. Grant in Horace Porter's
Campaigning with General Grant (p. 25)

Grant did his own work. Porter was amazed that he simply pushed a
finished page off the table onto the floor as he turned to the next, and
then, when finished, picked up the lot and sorted them. The commander of the armies of the West was his own file clerk. What he readied
for distribution were orders of great precision.

William S. McFeely
Grant: A Biography (p. 146)

Sometimes expedience must bow to details. Of course, the wisdom is to know when to get immersed in administrative details and
when to delegate. Good leaders know when *doing it themselves* is the
right thing to do.

Grant never missed an opportunity to propel events. His handwrit-
ten correspondence to his direct reports was usually written in a hurry,
in the field, and as he was thinking on his feet. He rarely dictated anything to Horace Porter because he knew he would have to edit the
order, even though he trusted Porter's administrative ability. Editing
meant adding a few more minutes to preparation, and Grant didn't
want to wait—not even on himself.

Grant refused to be swept up by drama, confusion, or surprise. He
had an uncanny awareness of process. If he had had telecommunica-
tions capability he would have used the phone or walkie-talkie to
issue orders. He would not have reduced action to inaction, progress
to status quo, striking a blow to receiving one.

INGENUITY

He depended for his success more upon the powers of invention than of adaptation.

Horace Porter
Campaigning with General Grant (p. 360)

Innovation is cumulative. Creative accomplishment is never the private, hidden breakthrough experience of one individual, but is an intricately shared experience without an identifiable moment of origin. It comes as a result of painstaking and loyal effort through time by people who have successfully *courted* the Muse and won enough of her favor to become the benefactor of a tidbit or two of insight. In today's economy, organizations either innovate or stagnate.

INTERNAL CUSTOMERS

⚬～⚬

To have a well-disciplined command, he did not deem it necessary to have an unhappy army.

> Horace Porter
> *Campaigning with General Grant* (p. 175)

Grant was handling his enemies within his own army with skill, but his Confederate enemies proved more difficult to outmaneuver.

> William S. McFeely
> *Grant: A Biography* (p. 125)

On that same day, March 6, 1862, Grant received a second stinging rebuke. Receiving this message was of course exceedingly painful for Grant, but he was in strong enough command of himself to read it closely and to strike back.

In a masterful telegram in his own defense, he stated that he had reported regularly to Halleck's chief staff officer, General Cullum, daily; if Cullum had failed to pass the information along to Halleck, it was not Grant's fault.

> William S. McFeely
> *Grant: A Biography* (p. 107–8)

Happy employees turn customers' smiles into symphonies. A disciplined service system itself is a product of the service culture. Because a service has no shelf life, each change to create a satisfied customer usually depends not so much on the competence of the service provider, but on his/her willingness to provide distinctive service. A loyal, but policy-driven customer-contact representative will probably infuriate customers. On the other hand, employees who feel happy and satisfied—and taken care of—generally become service ambassadors.

IRRECONCILABLE DIFFERENCES

[Chamberlain comments on how misleading field orders led to assumptions that confused his fellow officers and ended in a bizarre series of unproductive movements by Union forces] . . . As these apparently absurd performances involve again the action and honor of the Fifth Corps, it is proper to take them under examination. The accounts of the affair . . . given by General[s] Badeau . . . Grant . . . Sheridan . . . and Humphreys involve irreconcilable differences; and it is necessary to form our judgments . . . by taking into account the means of knowledge, and probably motives of action and of utterance, which to establish the credibility of witnesses.

Joshua Chamberlain
The Passing of the Armies (p. 185–86)

Sometimes the covers of a book are too far apart. Recognized for what they are, differences are usually differences in perception. Perceptions are based on attitudes. Attitudes on beliefs and values. Beliefs and values on socialization. Socialization on circumstance. Circumstance on fate or luck. Fate or luck on—well, you get the picture. Differences can be complicated and the forces that produced them complex.

Leaders finding themselves dealing with irreconcilable differences may be able to identify with Oscar Wilde's assessment of the irreconcilable nature of differences in viewpoint:

"Chuang Tzu was born in the fourth century before Christ. The publication of his book in English, two thousand years after his death, is obviously premature."[10]

One of the messages to leaders is to decide where you want to spend your energy. If the issue is important enough to warrant establishing "the credibility of witnesses," plan on using a mediator and, if circumstances necessitate, an arbitrator. One more thing, stay out of the middle because sometimes the covers of a book are too far apart.

LOYALTY

As I came near one of the regiments which was making preparations for the next morning's assault, I noticed that many of the soldiers had taken off their coats, and seemed to be engaged in sewing up rents in them. This exhibition of tailoring seemed rather peculiar at such a moment, but upon closer examination it was found that the men were calmly writing their names and home addresses on slips of paper, and pinning them on the backs of their coats, so that their dead bodies might be recognized upon the field, and their fate made known to their families at home. They were veterans who knew well from terrible experience the danger which awaited them, but their minds were occupied not with thoughts of shirking their duty, but with preparation for the desperate work of the coming morning. Such courage is more than heroic—it is sublime.

Horace Porter
Campaigning with General Grant (p. xvii–xviii)

. . . General Sheridan was not inclined to serve under any other commander but Grant . . .

Joshua Chamberlain
The Passing of the Armies (p. 101)

The prerequisite for loyalty is to love someone or something immensely. Loyalty, turned up a notch to sacrifice, is "more than heroic—it is sublime." Horace Porter's story above is one of the most gut-wrenching and touching accounts of loyalty and courage that appears in the annals of warfare. That kind of loyalty is rare. It is based on both courage and trust. The trust part comes from an inner knowing that senses the courageous act that must come is a necessary one. Most courageous acts come from a loyalty that places mission ahead of misery and cause before self. One of the greatest "exhibition[s] of tailoring" leaders can do is to customize work environments so that each employee's contributions and loyalty "might be recognized on up the field."

81

MANAGEMENT BY OBJECTIVES

———

When this was effected I felt a degree of relief scarcely ever equaled since. Vicksburg was not yet taken it is true, nor were its defenders demoralized by any of our previous moves. I was now in the enemy's country, with a vast river and the stronghold of Vicksburg between me and my base of supplies. But I was on dry ground on the same side of the river with the enemy. All the campaigns, labors, hardships and exposures from the month of December previous to this time that had been made and endured, were for the accomplishment of this one object.

U. S. Grant
The Personal Memoirs of Ulysses S. Grant (p. 284)

Objectives are tactical performance schematics. As such they are only expedient compasses drafted to guide movement toward defined ends. One thing all good leaders are aware of is that objectives are only means to ends, they are not ends in and of themselves. They are lamps along the way. When strategic goals change, tactics should change.

The power of any objective is measured by the resistance it attracts. An extraordinarily high belief in the value of an objective anchors both the desire and commitment to it, and that comes from the example modeled by the leader. There is no relationship—zero—between simply setting objectives and achieving increased productivity; however, there *is* a relationship between setting challenging but realistic objectives and improved performance. People will perform to the level of expectation expressed by a leader. Mark Sanborn, management consultant, shares this story:

"General H. Norman Schwarzkopf distinguished himself as a great leader during Operation Desert Storm. According to a story in Inc. magazine, early in his career he had been placed in charge of helicopter maintenance. When he asked how much of the helicopter unit was able to fly on any given day, he was told 75 percent. In tracking the performance of the unit, Schwarzkopf found that team members didn't come in at 74 percent or 76 percent, but always at 75 percent because '. . . that was the standard set for them.' Schwarzkopf told Inc. he decided to raise the team's sights. 'I said, I don't know anything about helicopter maintenance, but I'm establishing a new standard: 85 percent.' Within a short time, the team had lived up to the new expectation and 85 percent of the helicopters were flying each day."[11]

One of the most important psychological principles of objective setting is that the objective must be believable, reachable, and specific. Part of the believability is the legitimacy of the objective-giver. Is the leader believable? Are objectives doable? Reachable? They are *if* discriminating leaders know how to torque objectives just enough to elevate the standard of excellence to a level that exceeds the team's initial reach but not their grasp. When leaders push their people to meet a particularly challenging objective and succeed after concerted effort, they will feel a sense of satisfaction and "a degree of relief scarcely . . . equaled."

MANAGING CHAOS

But Grant was not thinking about attacking anyone just then. When Gordon had hit Sedgwick, only a mile from Grant's headquarters, the Wilderness Tavern command post had gone to pieces. At Meade's tent Grant tried to make sense of conflicting reports. Commanders were dashing up—"talking wildly and giving the most exaggerated reports," Porter thought—asking what they should do. Everyone was talking about "Lee, Lee." Grant stood first on one foot, then on the other, and finally went back to his own tent and sat on a chair. A field commander ran toward Grant. "General Grant," he said, winded from excitement, "this is a crisis that cannot be looked upon too seriously. I know Lee's methods well by past experience; he will throw his whole army between us and the Rapidan, and cut us off completely from our communications."

That brought Grant to his feet. He yanked the cigar out of his mouth and angrily raised his voice. "Oh, I am heartily tired of hearing about what Lee is going to do. Some of you always seem to think he is suddenly going to turn a double somersault, and land in our rear and on both of our flanks at the same time. Go back to your command, and try to think what we are going to do ourselves, instead of what Lee is going to do."

Anderson and Anderson
The Generals (p. 377)

One of Meade's staff men wrote that late in one day of heavy fighting, at about "half-past four what should Generals Grant and Meade take in their heads to do but, with their whole Staffs, ride into a piece of woods close to the front while heavy skirmishing was going on. We could not see a thing except our own men lying down; but there we sat on horseback while the bullets here and there came clicking among trunks and branches and an occasional shell added its discordant tone. I almost fancy Grant felt mad that things did not move faster, and so thought he would go sit in an uncomfortable place."

William S. McFeely
Grant: A Biography (p. 168)

Too many leaders subscribe to the rock/paper/scissors philosophy of running a business. When a crisis occurs, these reactionary leaders become as paralyzed as Rosecrans was at Chattanooga. They feverishly stoop to the ground, scoop up a handful of dust, and throw it into the air. Consequently they blind anyone who has some degree of competence in order to hide their own failure to see clearly.

A work environment that perpetuates crisis management cannot provide the stability for an effective performance-management system. Surrounded by outdated assumptions or suffocated from breathing their own stale exhaust, some managers are "driven from camp" by competitors. Today's economic realities demand leaders who have the guts to move about with unprecedented composure in chaos. Besides, chaos is nothing but excited order.

MERCENARY TASTES

Back of these orders lay the lesson [Grant] had learned in Missouri: the idea that in every battle there may come a moment when each side is fought out and ready to quit, and the belief that in such a moment victory will go to the side which is able to make one final effort. . . . What was important now was what happened in men's minds . . . Final victory would go to the side which insisted on winning it.

Bruce Catton
Grant Moves South (p. 168–69)

Extended effort is the conversion of resolve into action. The greatest, most heroic, most mercenary efforts have always been traceable to the love of praise. Oftentimes it is that one last push, that extra half-step, that last ounce of resolve that meets the objective and gains the victory. Effort creates events, but concentrated effort shapes events. Intention is the concept, but muscle is the reality. "Final victory [will] go to the [organization, team, leader] which [insists] on winning it."

MORALE

One cure for discontent was mail from home, and Grant took pains to make sure that his armies would get good postal service. . . . Even when troops were on the march, mail wagons trailed after them. . . . Another cure for discontent was work; work, together with some evidence that the work which was being done made sense.

Bruce Catton
Grant Moves South (p. 62–63)

Morale elevates the immune system of organizations. The "cure for discontent" is higher morale. The cure for low morale is high-principled, enthusiastic leadership. Low morale can exist with great leadership, but high morale cannot exist without it. The only way to boost morale is to lower complacency.

MOTIVATION

Scurrying to make defeat into victory, on May 30, 1863, [Grant] wrote a three-page order to his men exhorting them in spacious rhetoric to aspire to be martyrs equal to those of Monmouth and Bunker Hill and asking, "Shall not our flag float over Vicksburg? Shall not the great Father of Waters be opened to lawful commerce . . . "

William S. McFeely
Grant: A Biography (p. 132)

People tend to repeat behavior they are rewarded for. That statement initially appears to be too simplistic, too direct, too naive. To put all of motivation theory into one tiny encapsulated statement may seem ludicrous. Yet, it turns out to be the only sane comment to make about motivation. Simply reward what you want to see repeated. Establish the kind of work environment that literally compels spirited performance. Motivation is an inside job; it comes from a person's desire to accomplish something important, something *that* person wants to do. Anytime a leader attempts to *motivate* someone to do something the leader wants done (and experiences resistance from that someone), the result is manipulation—not motivation.

NEGOTIATION

General S. B. Buckner,
Confederate Army
Sir: Yours of this date, proposing armistice and appointment of commissioners to settle terms of capitulation, is just received. No terms except unconditional and immediate surrender can be accepted. I propose to move immediately upon your works.
I am, sir, very respectfully,
Your obedient servant,
U. S. GRANT,
Brigadier-General Commanding.

> Grant's response to Gen. Buckner's
> surrender request at Fort Donelson,
> February 16, 1862, The War of the
> Rebellion, Official Records

What General Lee's feelings were [at Appomattox] I do not know. As he was a man of much dignity, with an impassible face, it was impossible to say whether he felt inwardly glad that the end had finally come, or felt sad over the result, and was too manly to show it. Whatever his feelings, they were entirely concealed from my observation; but my own feelings, which had been quite jubilant on the receipt of his letter, were sad and depressed. I felt like anything rather than rejoicing at the downfall of a foe who had fought so long and valiantly, and had suffered so much for a cause though that cause was, I believe, one of the worst for which a people ever fought, and one for which there was the least excuse. I do not question, however, the sincerity of the great mass of those who were opposed to us.

> U. S. Grant
> *The Personal Memoirs of Ulysses S. Grant* (p. 629–30)

Both buyer and seller negotiate the sale. A knowledge of human behavior is essential to any negotiator. Few things could be simpler in definition or broader in scope than negotiation. Every want that demands satisfaction—and every need to be met—is at the least a forum for negotiation. There is one quality about negotiation that leaders must accept—negotiation isn't always neat, and more often than not isn't even nice. At best it is cooperative egotism. The best symbol, perhaps, of a negotiated settlement is a bridge. However, the strength of the negotiation helps determine what kind of bridge—pontoon, swinging bridge, drawbridge, or expansion bridge.

Negotiation is not a game—and it should not be entered into with the intention of crucifying the opponent. Its objective should not be a dead competitor. Leaders who ignore this last point risk it at their own peril. As successful negotiators, leaders must combine the alertness and speed of an expert swordsman with a politician's diplomacy. And like Grant, the negotiator who enjoys leverage must be prepared to thrust at the slightest opportunity and ask for "unconditional and immediate surrender."

On the other hand, the negotiator must be a sensitive artist, perceptive of even the slightest variation of color in an opponent's mood. At the correct moment, the consummate negotiator must be able to select from the multicolored palette exactly the right shades of compassion and tints of empathy that will lead to negotiation mastery. And like Grant, the winning negotiator will feel "like anything rather than rejoicing at the downfall of a foe who had fought so long and valiantly . . . "

NEW TECHNOLOGY

[His battlefield successes] were possible because Grant realized that weapon-power is the secret of tactics. He was not afraid to use the rifle, and he was not afraid to meet the rifle. Had he only carried this supreme understanding of what fighting demands to its logical conclusion, namely, that high superiority in weapon-power is ninety per cent of victory, he would have more fully realized the value of artillery, and have never ceased to call for more and more magazine rifles and carbines. What he did not understand, and what no general of his day understood, and few since have understood, was that the art of war had been revolutionized by the rifle, and to apply old tactics to new weapons, was tantamount to applying a whip to a locomotive.

J. F. C. Fuller
The Generalship of Ulysses S. Grant (p. 358–59)

Rapid change means faster technology transfer. The evidence is incontrovertible—organizations must embrace new technologies with open arms and open pocketbooks. Technologies, no matter how advanced, must support the service culture and product kingdoms. Too many organizations fail to embrace the new by clinging to the dilapidated old. When entrenched attitudes get in the way, reluctant leaders have a tough time making the kind of changes that lead to organizational growth and competitive health. As Richard Foster so aptly puts it:

"The past is prologue when people make the same mistakes and misjudgments about the future . . . It's more than the initial aversion we have to new technology like automated tellers; it's the fact that we may no longer be competent in the new world that technology brings. . . . We expect that the world will change, in fact [we] look forward to it, but somehow we don't think that it will affect us—our jobs, our businesses."[12]

It is relatively easy to spot emerging technologies on competitive horizons and to actually develop or redesign them. What is much more difficult, indeed agonizing at times, is to limit or abandon an older technology even though a little more progress is possible. People generally lose jobs, reorganizations occur, yet to paraphrase Fuller, to apply old tactics to new technologies is tantamount to applying a whip to a locomotive.

One of the common mistakes made by industry leaders is believing that there is plenty of time to ward off new technologies from naive competitors. However, rapid change means rapid technology transfer.

OBJECTIVITY

[Grant] never underrated himself in a battle; he never overrated himself in a report.

Horace Porter
Campaigning with General Grant (p. 361)

The victory was not to either party until the battle was over.

U. S. Grant
The Personal Memoirs of Ulysses S. Grant (p. 216)

Demand the credentials of all facts. Grant knew that the world was round and that the place that looks like the end may just be the beginning. He knew that the victory was not a reality until the reality was the victory. There is nothing so upsetting yet so appreciated as surgical objectivity.

ORDINARY

Of thirty-four new brigadiers named early in August, Grant ranked seventeenth, almost exactly in the middle; the same position, oddly enough, that he had occupied in his graduating class at West Point.

Henry Coppee
Life and Services of General U. S. Grant (p. 29)

Average doesn't mean ordinary! There's nothing ordinary about averaging a 10 percent increase in profit over a ten-year period—or averaging less than 1 percent turnover in personnel for the past fifteen years—or averaging a 22 percent reduction in time to first tangible test in product development over the last twenty-four months—or reducing the new project development cycle times on the average of 50 to 60 percent over the last three quarters. All of these productivity indicators are average, but they certainly aren't ordinary. Few organizations can accomplish them, let alone sustain them.

Grant ranked seventeenth out of thirty-four in his graduating class at West Point. He certainly fell in the average range, but to say his accomplishments were *ordinary* is to miss the point: average doesn't mean ordinary.

OUTSOURCING

⟡

Getting the necessary goods of war had been a problem for every general, and Congress was investigating charges of incompetence and fraud among army suppliers. As luck would have it, Grant's congressman was on the House Select Committee on Government Contracts, and Washburne arrived in Cairo on October 31, 1861, to investigate supply conditions. At the hearing, Grant explained that foreign guns presented problems because they were of a bore for which ammunition was not available in America; the bullets did not fit. Grant did not whine about ineptness in Washington, nor did he overstate the matter, but by the time he had finished, the purchase appeared to have been stupid, while he came through as intelligent.

William S. McFeely
Grant: A Biography (p. 85)

That same day Grant, frustrated and immobile, lashed out at the bustling activity of merchants who had rushed in to exploit both his soldiers and the civilians in the region . . . Grant was fed up with the cotton speculators and the greedy suppliers of goods to his armies.

William S. McFeely
Grant: A Biography (p. 123)

Grant was in position to crack down, here, partly because his quartermaster department had no funds, which meant that contractors could be paid only by voucher, and the vouchers had to have Grant's signed approval. Where prices seemed out of line, Grant would not sign. On one occasion he refused to approve a forage contract even though the Department quartermaster at St. Louis had endorsed it. When the indignant contractors displayed this officer's signature, Grant was unmoved:

"My reply to them was that they had got their contract without my consent, had got it approved against my sense of duty to the Government, and they might go on and deliver the forage and get their pay in the same way. I would not approve a voucher for them under that contract if they never got a cent. Hoped they would not. This forced them to abandon the contract and to sell the forage already delivered for what it was worth."

Bruce Catton
Grant Moves South (p. 94)

Perpetuating marginal resource availability is fanatical dieting with an outsourcing fetish. Effective supply management means effective internal controls to ensure quality and responsiveness. Qualification standards for vendors and suppliers must be specific, iron clad, and enforced. Like Grant, today's leaders need to "crack down" on contractors whose "prices seem out of line" and whose quality is suspect. Demand quality and get it or outsource to a more conscientious vendor.

PACING

In the beginning, Grant acted neither with the considered boldness of rushing his combat troops through the Wilderness nor with the rudimentary caution of keeping the army compactly grouped until his wagon train was well started southward. Instead the new commander-in-chief moved his groups on a timetable as if Lee's army were there merely to be acted upon, according to Grant's initiative.

Clifford Dowdey
Lee's Last Campaign (p. 131)

Be moderate in moderation. Pacing is essential in finishing anything. Moderation helps define useful toil. Grant had the luxury of escalation without usurpation. He felt in control. He had no need to hurry. Knowing when to apply pressure and release tension are excellent operational tools for leaders. Grant's moderation and steady advance toward Lee were not contradictions of his bias for action. They were complementary to it. He subordinated his penchant for quick decisive action to a reasonableness that sprung from an inner calm, a knowing that understood the relationship between pacing, momentum, and mass.

PATIENCE

In a letter to Sherman whose forces were outside of Savannah, Georgia: *Not liking to rejoice before the victory is assured, I abstain from congratulating you and those under your command, until bottom has been struck. I have never had a fear, however, for the result.*

U. S. Grant
The Personal Memoirs of Ulysses S. Grant (p. 559)

Run with patience. The secret of being patient is to do something else while you're waiting, and have no "fear . . . for the result." To paraphrase John Wesley, do what you can for as long as you can, wherever you are, with whatever you've got, long enough to be patient with the result. Once begun, let the process unfold the outcome. Always subordinate the predictable to the actual with patient, methodical, right action. The importance of this cannot be emphasized enough. Too many leaders fail to grasp that there is a point when patience becomes lethargy and indecisiveness. So run if you have to, and sprint if you must, with patience.

PATRIOTIC DISPATCH

The war has made us a nation of great power and intelligence. We have but little to do to preserve peace, happiness and prosperity at home, and the respect of other nations. Our experience ought to teach us the necessity of the first; our power secures the latter.

U. S. Grant
The Personal Memoirs of Ulysses S. Grant (p. 665)

Even global businesses operate within the borders of countries. Competition has linked many organizations of great power and global presence. We live in a global village, and it is inherent in the job of leaders to preserve technological superiority, service distinction, product quality, and employee job satisfaction—and the respect of other organizations. A leader's "experience ought to teach . . . the necessity of the first; (a leader's) power secures the latter."

PERSISTENCE

~~~

So Grant was alone; his most trusted subordinates besought him to change his plans, while his superiors were astounded at his temerity and strove to interfere. Soldiers of reputation and civilians in high places condemned, in advance, a campaign that seemed to them as hopeless as it was unprecedented. If he failed, the country would concur with the Government and the generals. That quiet confidence in himself which never forsook him, and which amounted indeed almost to a feeling of fate, was uninterrupted. Having once determined in a matter that required irreversible decision, he never reversed, nor even misgave, but was steadily loyal to himself and his plans. This absolute and implicit faith was, however, as far as possible from conceit or enthusiasm; it was simply a consciousness, or conviction, rather, which wrought the very strength it believed in; which was itself strength, and which inspired others with a trust in him, because he was able thus to trust himself.

Adam Badeau
Military History Of Ulysses S. Grant, Vol. 1 (p. 222)

In profiting by the Confederacy's faulty organization, this "Unconditional Surrender," Grant had shown himself to be an uncommonly pugnacious fighter. He drove. Nothing discouraged him and he never stopped trying. In his unspectacular, bulldog fashion, Grant had accomplished what had been expected of brilliant McClellan and of many another general of apparently superior gifts, who had also been presented by the Confederates with favorable conditions.

Clifford Dowdey
Lee's Last Campaign (p. 49)

If you pound on the door loud enough and long enough, you are certain to wake someone up. Once you decide to do something, achieve it at all costs of tedium or distaste. The gain in self-confidence after dispatching tiresome labor is immense. So lead on, roughshod if need be—in Grant's bulldog fashion or with finesse as circumstances allow. But lead on. Persevere. Persist. Lead out of a consciousness of conviction.

POLITICALLY INCORRECT

The result was tragic, because what was needed after the Civil War—after any great war—was a man who could transcend the national character. Instead of transcending it, Grant embodied it. [Grant's] genius had been that he could compel men to be themselves. He could not make them surpass themselves and that was what this time called for.

Bruce Catton commenting on Grant's
election to president in
*America Goes to War: An Introduction to the
Civil War and Its Meaning to Americans Today* (p. 112)

Rank is a great leveler. The truth is Grant used all of his native intelligence and physical capacities to their greatest extent. He literally pushed his professional envelope. It was Grant's silent, unassuming productivity that made him famous. However, as with Grant, once you climb to the top of success—and competency—nothing recedes like success.

POWER

—◆◇◆—

[Grant] knew something of what does and does not accompany power.

J. F. Packard
*Grant's Tour Around the World,
with Incidents of His Journey Through
England, Ireland, and Scotland* (p. 64)

Power has its residence in dependency. Essentially the essence of leadership is influence over followers. However, the influence process between *leader* and *led* is not unidirectional. Influence is always reciprocal. Therefore power is always dependent on influence.

There is no neutral ground from which to construct notions about power because in leadership terms, it is loaded with emotional content. Power, it appears, arises out of the interplay between influence and dependency. The drives to fill needs and employ means are real. Using influence and dependency as parentheses, factors such as an organization's permeability, adaptability, differentiation, and integration fall somewhere along the linear equation of power. Each of these aspects is affected by the character of power. Power in the wrong hands can destroy an organization's ability to produce anything substantial.

The types of influences that "accompany power" are: legitimate requests (formal authority), instrumental compliance (rewards), coercion (threats or force), rational persuasion (personal magnetism), rational faith (believability), inspirational appeal (ideology), indoctrination (affiliation), and information distortion (access to vital information). The extent to which each of those is used depends on how influential the leader is. How influential the leader is determines how powerful the leader remains.

It is not power that corrupts leaders, but the absence of leaders that corrupts power. Grant knew that power is the opium of leadership in the sense that it allows management to command ends without enduring the means.

PRACTICALITY

It has been said more than once that General Grant had not the gift of imagination. It is true that he had not that kind of imagination that sees an enemy where none exists; that multiplies by five the number of those who happened to be in his front; that discovers obstacles impossible to overcome whenever there is a necessity to act; that sees the road open and the way clear to victory when the foe is far away and not threatening; that conjures up, on his near approach, a multitude of impossible movements being made on the flanks and on the rear; that sets the brain of a commander into a whirl of doubt and uncertainty which generally ends in a hasty retreat or ignominious defeat . . .

Colonel Bruce in J. F. C. Fuller's
The Generalship of Ulysses S. Grant (p. 378)

He had little of the poet in his composition and much of the mechanic, in that he was extremely practical, accepting situations rather than creating them, and working without complaint with the means he had at hand.

J. F. C. Fuller
The Generalship of Ulysses S. Grant (p. 417)

The night march had been a triumphant procession for the new commander. Grant had never been cheered like that, but he just grumped to his staff about the most unfortunate uproar, which would give away the move.

Anderson and Anderson
The Generals (p. 380)

I congratulated Sheridan upon his recent great victory and had a salute of a hundred guns fired in honor of it, the guns being aimed at the enemy around Petersburg.

U. S. Grant
The Personal Memoirs of Ulysses S. Grant (p. 536)

Practicality is centrifugal thought intensified around the parameters of a problem. Assumptions, hunches, and guesses cannot

103

keep pace with the realities of practicality. Leaders who put too much faith in cold theories and pregnant concepts will need to pay more attention to the objectivity of practical experiences. Too many young managers sequester themselves from the reality of work by remaining in offices with terrific views of the skyline instead of practicing visible leadership in the trenches.

Reason's cash value, in experimental terms, is practicality. Evaluation and investigative analysis are the labors of reason. Assumptions must be exposed, delusions sifted through, the promptings of the entrepreneurial spirit examined by the voice of reason. Detailed, computerized data collection systems, paper-pencil inventories, and trend analysis programs create a data trail that adds to practicality's cash value. One of a leader's top priorities has to be coming to grips with reality—as opposed to politics, impressions, postures, and all the staff managing that goes on within the organization. How else can leaders see through apparitions manufactured in someone's mind like: "an enemy where none exists . . . obstacles impossible to overcome . . . a multitude of impossible movements being made on the flanks and on the rear?" That's why managers must follow Grant's lead and refuse to be caught up in a world of abstractions by staying in the trenches with the troops long enough to make decisions based on processed reality.

PROCESS CHAMPION

. . . Grant had a remarkable sense of the whole of the event. It was always changing; nothing was ever settled. His perception was not a single snapping of the shutter to give a brilliantly clear image of a battle stopped in full clarity. Instead what he saw always included a dimension of time, an awareness of the unfolding evolving motion of the life of the war . . .

The single, splendid, climactic effort was not the reality of war as Grant understood it. He never expected to get caught up with his work . . . He knew that each day, and each battle, led to the next. The way to reach ultimate victory was to develop a stronger sense of war's rhythm . . .

William S. McFeely
Grant: A Biography (p. 103)

Balance sheets fail to measure the invisible equity. Management thinking in most parts of the global village is currently trapped in the old manufacturing model of enterprise. That is, the old model monitors financial performance carefully, maximizes profitability by conservation of *everything,* concentrates on predefined normative measures of employee performance, and sees people as movable assets to be managed like any other capital asset. According to H. Thomas Johnson and Robert S. Kaplan: " . . . most of the accounting practices of today evolved to meet the demands of people outside the corporation for information. Investors, governments, regulators, and financial analysts all want 'hard' information: monetary measures of assets that can be traded on the market. Even though the real selling price of a business is usually higher than the book value of its assets to the extent of its 'invisible equity' such as the value of patents, image, and reputation, experience of its work force, skill of its management, and the like, the balance sheet shows only tangible assets that can be produced in an audit."[13]

Asset management isn't complete without an accounting of the rhythm, "an awareness of the unfolding . . . motion of the life of the [organization]." It will require watching the customer more carefully, concentrating on customer interface and service outcomes, assessing moments of truth up and down the internal service ladder, leading through example, protecting the loyal customer base, reporting sales and earnings on an annual basis, etc. The role of the service leaders in the twenty-first century will be one of process champion and service ambassador. These champions will emphasize both building real value and conserving assets.

PROFANITY

I never learned to swear . . . I could never see the use of swearing . . . I have always noticed . . . that swearing helps to rouse a man's anger.

U. S. Grant
Campaigning with General Grant (p. 177)

I am not aware of ever having used a profane expletive in my life; but I would have the charity to excuse those who may have done so, if they were in charge of a train of Mexican pack mules at the time.

U. S. Grant in William S. McFeely's
Grant: A Biography (p. 33)

Yet Dana could see no cracks in the man's control. He recalled one night riding beside Grant in black darkness; Grant's horse stumbled and nearly pitched the General into the mud, and Dana found himself thinking, "Now he will swear." Grant disappointed him. He regained control of his horse and went on with his ride without giving any sign of impatience or irritation, and Dana reflected afterward that from one end of the campaign to the other he never heard Grant use an oath.

Hamlin Garland
in William S. McFeely's
Grant: A Biography (p. 420–21)

Profanity is nothing more than a vulgar descendant of Neanderthal grunts. However you choose to label it, vulgarity, unparliamentary or indelicate language, obscenity, cursing, or being foulmouthed, it all amounts to the same thing—conversational litter. Leaders who use it are suffering from delusions of its relevance.

PROJECT MANAGEMENT

The march of Sherman's army from Atlanta to the sea and north to Goldsboro, while it was not accompanied with the danger that was anticipated, . . . had an important bearing, in various ways, upon the great object we had in view, that of closing the war.

U. S. Grant
The Personal Memoirs of Ulysses S. Grant (p. 651–52)

There is no insignificant work—only insignificant effort. It is the action quotient that brings projects to a close, not the planning quotient. Pick projects big enough to matter and small enough to complete. The most important function of project management on any level is to complete the project on time, using economy of resources and rewarding the right performance. This is the basic architecture of project management; the rest is ornamentation and decoration of structure.

PROFESSIONAL COURTESY

Despite social strains, Grant continued to seek our plantation house porches for rest. At Guiney Station, he visited a farm and was entertained by a woman who shared an important piece of information. Did Grant know, she asked, that Stonewall Jackson had died in that very house? Grant sat through a lengthy description of mighty Stonewall's final days, final hours, final minutes, and final words. Shifting from one side to another in his chair—he still had the boils—he said something about Jackson's being a "sterling, manly cadet" and beat a retreat to his headquarters.

Agassiz
Meade's Headquarters 1863–1865:
*Letters of Colonel Theodore Lyman from
The Wilderness to Appomattox* (p. 132–33)

Civility costs absolutely nothing yet compounds interest. Grant applied the oil of politeness to the lamp of hospitality. He knew it is better to use courtesy than offend the host or hostess. His polite concession allowed him to "beat a [gracious] retreat to his headquarters." Leaders can follow Grant's example in the exercise of a little etiquette. After all, professional courtesy is your public face; what you are thinking is your business.

PURPOSEFUL IMPATIENCE

There was a spur on the heel of every order [Grant] sent, and his subordinates were made to realize that in battle it is the minutes which control events.

Horace Porter
Campaigning with General Grant (p. 58)

Now we realized the effects of Grant's permission to "push things,"—some of these things being ourselves. It was much better to be on top and . . . know what there was beyond . . . I thought of Grant and his permission to "push things" . . .

Joshua Chamberlain
The Passing of the Armies (p. 225, 236)

The one great virtue that marked General Grant's character as superior to others was that in proportion to his increased responsibility and care came increased ability to act, increased power to meet the emergency.

Bruce Catton
Grant Moves South (p. 108)

This was supremely characteristic. Shiloh had been fought, it had been won, and then and always Grant's idea was to get on with the war without wasting time on the backward glance or on a long counting of the cost.

Bruce Catton
Grant Moves South (p. 264)

Work tirelessly to free people from needless restrictions that handcuff performance. Organizations must be performance-driven and impatient with less than desirable results. Few organizations offer valid *driving* licenses. Every managerial act must be seen as an unequivocal support for urgency in pursuit of constant testing, change, and improvement. Sometimes leaders seem impatient with any kind of results, particularly if the progress isn't visible at first glance. Good leaders recognize that there is visible accomplishment and invisible accomplishment. The wisdom of evaluating the true nature of work and achievement is *knowing* the work to be done through experience. Knowing *about* something is not the same thing as knowing the *essence of* something.

REDUNDANCY

Two commanders on the same field are always one too many. I believe now that there would have been no more battles of the West after the capture of Fort Donelson if all the troops in that region had been under a single commander who would have followed up that victory.

U. S. Grant
The Personal Memoirs of Ulysses S. Grant (p. 132, 253)

Redundancy is overemphasizing unnecessary duplication too often by exaggerating surpluses. To say anything more about redundancy would be redundant. So avoid it whenever you can.

RE-ENGINEERING

A similar fate befell the new hope kindled by Grant's sudden change to a new ease of operations—a movement bold if not hazardous, being practically a change of front under fire for the whole army on a grand scale.

Joshua Chamberlain
The Passing of the Armies (p. 3–4)

The biggest drawback to re-engineering is that some leaders want to change everything—or nothing. Re-engineering is a total quality management process that involves a fundamental rethinking and radical redesign of complex business processes to achieve dramatic and sustainable improvements in critical, contemporary performance measures such as cost, service, quality, reliability, and responsiveness.

Re-engineering programs should be safe havens where ruthless examination of organizational realities will not become distorted by the politics of the moment or inhibited by the cowardice of top management to make the necessary changes and own the results.

REGRETS

I have always regretted that the last assault at Cold Harbor was ever made . . . no advantage whatever was gained to compensate the heavy loss we sustained.

U. S. Grant
The Personal Memoirs of Ulysses S. Grant (p. 503)

Grant was not the only one who didn't want to talk about Cold Harbor . . . Called the *Golgotha of American history* it did not excite the participants' Victorian need to describe as did other major battles of the Civil War. A line here, a reference there, a paragraph tucked into voluminous reminiscence were all the chroniclers could bring themselves to write.

Anderson and Anderson
The Generals (p. 400–401)

Grant . . . confessed that there were only two days of battle that he regretted: June 3, 1864 at Cold Harbor, and this day in May outside Vicksburg. He saw men agonizingly reach the top of the enemy's earthworks, only to be driven back [by] murderous fire.

William S. McFeely
Grant: A Biography (p. 132)

Regrets are exhumed remorse excavated as apologies. We all make mistakes. All of us have things we'd like to forget. The remedy—the only sane approach—is forgiveness, for the pain you may have caused and the pain you may be going through.

Truly forgive yourself for the reorganization you botched. Pardon yourself for chewing out that direct report in the presence of his colleagues. Forgive yourself for not taking better care of your health. Have mercy on yourself for the harsh words screamed at that sales clerk. Stop punishing yourself for not spending more time with your family or that special someone. Release from your mind that boardroom outburst. Ask forgiveness from those you believe you have offended—including yourself.

RESOURCE ALLOCATION

—◆—

... I think [the] correct definition of great generalship regards not so much the power to command resources, but the ability to ... handle successfully ... the economy ... of the expenditure of force ... the ability to account the cost ... and to discriminate between probabilities ... the ability to judge characters. [Sometimes] he was rather critical in his estimates of subordinates ... [Rank] may be applied ... to control resources, and conquer by main force.

Joshua Chamberlain
The Passing of the Armies (p. 379–80)

The war was taking on its final character: it was no longer a mere matter of armies, but of two nations putting every resource into a struggle for survival. All of the capacities which the country possessed were to be used remorselessly, to the hilt, until the enemy's ability to fight had been destroyed.

William S. McFeely
Grant: A Biography (p. 404–5)

Allow people fiduciary guardianship of allocated resources. Leaders depend on people to use the resources they have been provided—wisely and with discretion. Most of the time, however, management is too cautious in giving people the authority they need to procure and use allocated resources. So one of the definitions of great leadership "regards not so much the power to command resources, but the ability to ... handle successfully ... the economy ... of the expenditure ... " That has always been the rub. Leaders provide resources (that's their job) but then handcuff people with needless restrictions associated with expenditures and procurements. It boils down to an issue of trust. In his book *A Passion for Excellence,* Tom Peters shares a story every manager and leader should hear:

"This is typical of what we found: The first-line supervisor was responsible for some twenty-five to thirty-five people, and had $1 million at least, and often up to $4 million worth of capital equipment, under her or his control. And yet, characteristically, this supremely responsible individual didn't have the authority to buy an $8.95 can of paint to clean up his or her people's work space."

"There comes a special time when we weep at the $8.95 paint-bucket . . . we spent a pleasant afternoon over a bottle or so of wine talking about their experiences with allowing their people a little bit more control. There's one story that we remember particularly clearly. This executive, we'd judge in his late fifties, was coming late to this subject of treating people with respect. The experiment he launched consisted of taking a couple of his facilities—an old plant and a foundry—and giving them $2,000 a month apiece to spend any way they wished. There were only two strictures: the plant manager could not sit on the committee that decided on the nature of the expenditure, and the composition of the expenditure committee had to mirror the proportion of managerial to nonmanagerial people in the facility's population. He recalled the first month of the experiment. He'd granted the $2,000. The likely nature of the expenditure had been the subject of much flippant chatter among the senior people, several of whom thought our friend was a bit batty ("They'll buy handguns"). What did the people in those old facilities choose to do? Well, one group took the $2,000 and built a memorial garden outside the plant. It honored past members of the work force who, over the course of several decades, had died in industrial accidents and in foreign wars.

"Yes, these are the same beings of a lower order who are not responsible enough to spend $8.95 wisely. Yet, given $2,000, what do they do with it? Buy handguns? No, a memorial garden for former colleagues. And that is the nature of the average human being in the work force, if given an opportunity to shine."[14]

RETREAT FORWARD

This was an instance of [Grant's] marked aversion to turning back, which amounted almost to a superstition. He often put himself to the greatest personal inconvenience to avoid it. When he found he was not traveling in the direction he intended to take, he would try all sorts of cross-cuts, ford streams, and jump any number of fences to reach another road rather than go back and take a fresh start.

Horace Porter
Campaigning with General Grant (p. 73)

I shall take no backward steps . . .

U. S. Grant in Horace Porter's
Campaigning with General Grant (p. 82)

Always retreat forward. It is no disgrace to start over again—only begin from where you *are,* not from where you *were.*

RETURN ON INVESTMENT

———✦———

The striking fact is thus established that we had more men killed and wounded in the first six months of Grant's campaign, than Lee had at any one period of it in his whole army. The hammering business had been hard on the hammer.

Joshua Chamberlain
The Passing of the Armies (p. 10)

No amount of salary, benefits, or stock options will compensate for neglecting your people. There are two times in your career as a leader when employees should not be laid off unnecessarily, fired without cause, discriminated against because they're *different,* hammered because they ask unsettling questions, or intentionally stressed beyond repair—when you cannot afford to lose them, and when you can.

REVERSE ANGLE

Grant confessed, there was no engineer officer to lay out fortifications and he himself had forgotten what little West Point had taught him about this art; and "I have no desire to gain a 'Pillow notoriety' for a branch of service that I have forgotten all about." The reference was to the Confederacy's General Gideon Pillow, who commanded something styled vaguely an "army of liberation" in the extreme southeast corner of the state; an inept, quarrelsome soldier who, in the Mexican War, had won derision by building a fortified line with the ditch on the wrong side.

Bruce Catton
Grant Moves South (p. 34)

Better to succumb to pillow talk than Pillow notoriety. So often managers attempt to live and work backwards; then try to have more things (technologies, perks, franchises, empires) in order to do more of what they want (evaluate trend analyses, corner markets, produce products, hire employees, invest), believing they will be more fulfilled or happier. All that route will gain them is a little "Pillow notoriety." It takes them 180 degrees in the opposite direction. It turns out to be a counterclockwise movement into ulcers, heart attacks, and failure. They have reversed—Pillowed—the order of lasting happiness and success.

The way it actually works is this: leaders must first start with *who* they really are (analytical, compassionate, maverick, visionary, family-focused, high-energy, reserved, methodical, loner), then do what they need to do (invent, evaluate, empathize, risk, spend quality time, exercise regularly, plan) in order to have what they want (innovation, precision, satisfied customers, winning against the odds, enjoying friends and family, feeling good).

RISK ASSESSMENT

The day after Fort Henry fell, Grant went with his staff and a cavalry escort to take a look at the far more important Fort Donelson, 11 miles downstream. Donelson was garrisoned by some 15,000 rebel troops, the same number available to Grant. The textbooks uniformly said a besieging force should outnumber the besieged by five to one. But attacking anyway, Grant proved that a commander's actions win wars—not textbooks.

Gene Smith
Lee and Grant (p. 113)

Leaders who swear it can't be done count the risk, not the gain. A tight-fisted, white-knuckled grip on the familiar can keep leaders and organizations from reaching out and grasping a more competitive tomorrow. Most risks, calculated or not, are simply ego risks. In order to master the uncertainties associated with risk, philosophers meditate, sports trainers medicate, politicians insulate, and leaders hibernate—in ivory towers. There is a time for assessing risk. Calculated risks keep leaders from taking "bet-the-business" chances. You can't cross an abyss in two small jumps. Every great risk has a halfway point, a recognizable glitch, a split second when it can be recalled, canceled, or remedied. Once that point is past (in physics it's called the *bifurcation point*, the point of transformation or demise), the time for assessment is over. All your energy must go into the *doing*.

RUMOR

. . . from the disgruntled contractors themselves there came plenty. Stories that Grant was drinking heavily began to circulate . . .

Bruce Catton
Grant Moves South (p. 95)

Rumor and gossip are conversational compost. What some invent, ignorance enlarges. Those who gossip congregate, like a coroner's inquest, to feast on the murdered reputations of the *departed.* Character assassinations are the opiate of a gossiper's demise of friendships.

SECOND GUESSING

Ifs defeated the Confederates . . .

U. S. Grant
The Personal Memoirs of Ulysses S. Grant (p. 215)

Ifs have no clout. Ifs, oughts, and should haves are useless devices employed to justify unheeded lessons learned from past experience. Once something has occurred—a missed opportunity, a fruitless business venture, a failed marriage, a miscalibration, a wrong turn, a customer service bottleneck—it is useless to offer excuses. Leaders who *should* on themselves and *should* on others are putting people in a double-bind situation. Ifs are fruitless attempts to push rewind buttons, to reverse irreversible human events. Ifs have defeated more than Confederates. They have ruined many a career and destroyed many a leader.

SELF-CONFIDENCE

The place where Harris had been encamped a few days before was still there and the marks of a recent encampment were plainly visible, but the troops were gone. My heart resumed its place. It occurred to me at once that Harris had been as much afraid of me as I had been of him. This was a view of the question I had never taken; but it was one I never forgot afterwards. From that event to the close of the war, I never experienced trepidation upon confronting an enemy, though I always felt more or less anxiety. I never forgot that he had as much reason to fear my forces as I had his. The lesson was valuable. . . .

I felt some hesitation in suggesting rank as high as the colonelcy of a regiment, feeling somewhat doubtful whether I would be equal to the position. But I had seen nearly every colonel who had been mustered in from the State of Illinois, and some from Indiana, and felt that if they could command a regiment properly, and with credit, I could also.

U. S. Grant
The Personal Memoirs of Ulysses S. Grant (p. 144)

Men who met him for the first time in late 1863 got to know a different Grant from the uncertain captain who left Galena. Adam Badeau, who joined Grant as secretary, said his new boss "had no fear of not doing all that he was put in his place to do. He did not know, he said, how long it might be before he accomplished his task, nor what interruptions or obstacles might intervene, but of its eventual accomplishment no shadow of a doubt ever seemed to cross his mind." Another subordinate said Grant was "very far from being a modest man, as the word modest is generally understood. . . . His absolute confidence in his own judgment upon any subject which he had mastered added to his accurate estimate of his own ability."

Anderson and Anderson
The Generals (p. 353)

Ultimately self-confidence is self-approval. There is genius within and courage and strength and answers. Leaders, as people themselves, don't see things so much as *things* are; leaders see things as *leaders* are. It is no exaggeration to say that self-confidence is a magical talisman. Eleanor Roosevelt's certainty about the subject of self-confidence serves as confirmation: "No one can make you feel inferior without your consent."[15] Some of the greatest victories leaders will have are those over self-doubt, self-ridicule, and self-punishment.

SENSE OF HUMOR

Back on the porch after lunch Grant looked quizzically into the sudden question of a reporter. How long, the newspaperman asked, will it take you to get to Richmond? Grant took the cigar out of his mouth and paused. "I will agree to be there in about four days. That is, if General Lee becomes a party to the agreement. But if he objects, the trip will undoubtedly be prolonged." A ripple of relieved laughter played through the staff. But Grant was only half joking. He wanted to get through northern Virginia as quickly as possible. He knew Lee would try to block his path.

Anderson and Anderson
The Generals (p. 366–67)

To appreciate nonsense implies a serious interest in making life work. What made Grant's sense of humor work was that it didn't presume to teach or profess to preach at anyone. Laughter is a cleansing agent for life's serious side. Grant used it well as a tea-kettle response to relieve the pressures associated with command. Well-timed humor is just as effective a productivity tool as Pareto analysis, zero defects quality measures, and just-in-time inventory tracking systems. No, actually it's much more effective—it doesn't take as long to reduce slippage and induce spirited performance.

SIMPLICITY

No matter how vigorously the drummer beat the cadence, Grant couldn't, or wouldn't, march in time. No ear, he said, explaining that he knew but two songs. "One is Yankee Doodle, the other isn't." Men who knew Grant only from press reports were surprised to find him so small. They were further surprised by his voice, which was soft and musical and exceedingly clear. His manner—reserved, cordial, and shy—disarmed individuals prepared to dislike him. Theodore Lyman wrote that Grant was a "man of natural, severe simplicity, in all things—the very way he wears his high-crowned felt hat shows this: He neither puts it on behind his ears, nor draws it over his eyes; much less does he cock it on one side, but sets it straight and very hard on his head. His riding is the same; without the slightest 'air' and, *per contra,* without affectation of homeliness; he sits firmly in the saddle and looks straight ahead, as if only intent on getting to some particular point." Grant "talks bad grammar," said Lyman, "but he talks it naturally, as much as to say, 'I was so brought up and, if I try fine phrases I shall only appear silly.' " He demonstrated only three emotions, Lyman thought—"deep thought; extreme determination; and great simplicity and calmness."

Anderson and Anderson
The Generals (p. 361)

He is one of the Americans who have given us a language for simple things, important things. We need it for the immense task of making common ground with men like those who understood him, and marched with him, and killed for him.

William S. McFeely
Grant: A Biography (p. 514)

Noble simplicity is an adornment. To those who really knew him, Ulysses S. Grant had deep pockets of emotional strength tucked away in his simplicity. The price most leaders pay for today's technological, economical, and global complexity is too high. When you think about all the effort it takes to make things work—to alter even the slightest bit of customer perceptions or raise employee morale—you are left pining for the straightforwardness of primitive peoples and for some modicum of physical, get-your-hands-dirty work. Simplicity is really sophistication, an operational refinement. It is an adornment to those, like Grant, who have filled their lives with great deeds.

SITUATIONAL LEADERSHIP

The presidency of Ulysses S. Grant makes one of the haunting stories of American history. It is a tragic story—tragic both for Grant and for the country—for it shows a great man and a great nation confronting a profound and complex set of problems. . . . In the Spring of 1865 and for some time thereafter, he was probably the best-liked, most completely trusted man in the United States. Once Lincoln was gone he seemed to stand for everything Lincoln had stood for; . . . Choosing him in 1868, the nation simply confided in its own native genius. In this man who represented the great average so perfectly, it found one who, like the country itself, had been able to function at complete capacity in the turmoil of war.

Bruce Catton
America Goes to War: An Introduction to the Civil War and Its Meaning to Americans Today (p. 106–9)

. . . in the light of the history of the Army of the Potomac, it is hard to escape the conclusion . . . that [it] lacked the one great ingredient for success: grim, ferocious, driving force at the top. Grant had it, to be sure . . .

Bruce Catton
America Goes to War: An Introduction to the Civil War and Its Meaning to Americans Today (p. 85)

Lincoln's letter, with its grasp of essentials, makes it clear that he perceived Grant as a pivotal figure—as a fighter eager for a fight.

William S. McFeely
Grant: A Biography (p. 104)

. . . Grant was necessary to bringing that war to a close . . . His power to wield force to the bitter end, must entitle him to rank high as a commanding general. His concentration of energies, inflexible purpose, unselfishness, patience, and imperturbable long-suffering, his masterly reticence, ignoring . . . advice on criticism, his magnanimity in all relations, but more than all—his infinite trust in the final triumph of his cause, set him apart and alone above the others.

Joshua Chamberlain
The Passing of the Armies (p. 381)

Far down inside, perhaps, it was what he had always wanted. No one knew this general as well as his wife, Julia, and she saw him as the born fighter. Many years later she summed up his feeling about the army by writing: "He was happy in the fight and the din of battle, but restless in the barracks . . . He could no more resist the sound of a fife or a drum or a chance to fire a gun than a woman can resist bonets."

David M. Pletcher
*Rails, Mines and Progress: Seven
American Promoters in Mexico* (p. 181)

Leadership competence is inextricably linked to role competence. The fusion of a leader's experience, education, personality, and talents with circumstance and timing determine leadership worth. Leadership competence is contextual competence. Although there is no one best leadership style, there are certain qualifications, traits, and competencies that seem to make leaders more effective in particular situations. Both Lincoln and Julia Grant saw Grant as a "fighter eager for a fight"—"happy in the fight and din of battle but restless in the barracks." It comes as no surprise that Grant was much more effective as a military presence than as a political leader.

Using a biological metaphor, all living things go through cycles of birth, development, maturation, and decline. Organizations go through similar cycles or patterns of development. The success or failure of any leader depends on how well that leader's competencies match the growth cycle of the organization. A mismatch between a leader's fit and the organization's direction can spell disaster for both leader and organization. The history of leaders, renowned and dismissed, and organizations large and small, confirms the direct relationship between the role leaders are asked to play and the organization's developmental cycle into which that leader is thrust.

Grant, "who represented the great average so perfectly . . . had been able to function at complete capacity in the turmoil of war." His *fit* in the Presidency wasn't quite as good, however. The nation was convulsing. It was going through withdrawal after the Civil War. It was writhing in pain for shooting itself in the foot. It was going through massive restructuring and renewal. It needed a leader who was a mover and shaker, an organizational alchemist, one who could handle the corrupt political machinery that saw, in the wounded America, limitless economic opportunities for personal and political gain.

The timing wasn't right for Grant. He was too compliant, too accepting of the circumstances in which he found himself. Like many other mismatched leaders today, he found himself in the wrong job, at the wrong time, with the wrong credentials and the wrong team of people. Grant would have made a much better president in an organization that was in a mature, stable cycle of development. His meticulous nature, eye for detail, and bias for action would have moved the organization toward changes in technology and markets that would have been healthy.

Leaders who are good administrators and bureaucrats will be happier and more productive in organizations that are stable, mature, and conventional. Organizations that are making the switch from start-up or renewal to stabilization and balance need leaders who focus on quality initiatives through continuous improvement and total quality management. Leaders who are visionaries and crusaders for change are best suited for organizations on the verge of start-up or reorganization. To take any leader out of his/her natural element (competency niche) limits the leader's overall effectiveness and diminishes contributions that would otherwise "entitle [him/her] to rank high as a commanding general."

SOLE RESPONSIBILITY

His responsibility isolates him. That Grant learnt this supreme lesson during a morning's march, and in face of a vacant camp, shows that in this man there was something outside the common. He could learn; he could analyze his fears, he could make them speak to him. Because he was a student of his own errors and weaknesses, much more so than an illumined genius, we see this man through toil and tribulation defeating his own ignorance, and "keeping right on" to the very end.

J. F. C. Fuller
The Generalship of Ulysses S. Grant (p. 75)

As leaders, let our object be our company, our whole company, and nothing but our company. Leaders are responsible for actions performed in response to circumstances of which they have no knowledge. Jean-Paul Sartre sums it up quite nicely: "I am responsible for everything . . . except for my very responsibility, for I am not the foundation of my being. Therefore everything takes place as if I were compelled to be responsible. I am abandoned in all the world . . . in the sense that I find myself suddenly alone and without help, engaged in a world for which I bear the whole responsibility without being able, whatever I do, to tear myself away from this responsibility for an instant."[16]

STRATEGY

Grant was not born to win the Civil War—he trained himself to win it, and in his training myths played a small part. By close observation and reflection, he brought himself to realize the interdependence of politics and strategy; and not until present-day statesmen create a grand strategy of peace as Grant created a grand strategy of war, that is a relationship between national politics and international affairs, will a solution to world difficulties be discovered, and a line of direction established between the pressure and resistance of these two.

J. F. C. Fuller
The Generalship of Ulysses S. Grant (p. 411)

In his assessment of the battle, Grant gave credit to Confederate President Jefferson Davis for an asset to the Union victory . . .

Grant had a very low opinion of Davis's capacity as a military strategist and wrote caustically of the "several occasions during the war" when Davis "came to the relief of the Union army by means of his superior military genius."

William S. McFeely
Grant: A Biography (p. 148–49)

Leadership is not a spectator sport. The art and science of effective leadership is the ability to focus effort and guide people in the right direction. One of the best ways to do that is to stay tuned in to both internal and external customer needs and do what it takes to create value for your services and products in the eyes of the *beholder.* Once you know what *customers* want, *you'll* want to develop a strategy to give it to them.

Leaders influence mind-sets by creating strategies that compel performance and magnetize customers. It will come as no surprise to leaders who lead their industries that every successful organization can point to one or more value-added strategies that solved a customer's problem and drove their buying decisions. Basically, all strategy seeks to create a template for competitive advantage. Competitive advantage seeks to provide comparable buyer value more efficiently than hungry competitors (lower cost) or perform business activities at comparable cost with attention directed at creating more perceived value than competitors, and thus enjoy a premium price (differentiation). Good strategy will attempt to ensure, then sustain, a competitive advantage by smoothing out the rough edges in its cycle of service or *value chain.* Leaders who want to strengthen the value chain will have to start with a vision that is as compelling as Father Theodore Hesburgh's conception of one: "It's got to be a vision you articulate clearly and forcefully . . . you can't blow an uncertain trumpet."[17]

STRUGGLE

—————

The old American note sounds in them [Ulysses and Julia Grant],
the sense of the "hard" life and the plain speech.

Henry James on Grant's
letters in William S. McFeely's
Grant: A Biography (p. 518)

Struggle is the masterpiece of survival. Grant's struggle epito-
mizes America's struggle to set oneself free from the limits one is
born into, learn something of the value of those limits, and rise above
them to meet new limits. He was an honor student in "the hard life
and the plain speech." Grant *knew* that in a serious struggle (like the
Civil War had become) there is no worse cruelty than being magnani-
mous too soon. Once he broke the South the time for magnanimity
came at Appomattox.

Leaders, the survivors, *know* that life and work are struggles. They
know that every good and decent thing in the world stands each con-
secutive moment of now on the razor edge of disaster and must be
fought for—and earned—whether it's an idea, a value, a market, or
global presence.

TACTICS

General Grant evidently intended to rely more on tactics than strategy . . . in a personal letter to General Sherman on March 22d, . . . "I shall start out with no distinct view, further than holding Lee's forces from following Sheridan. But I shall be along myself, and will take advantage of anything that turns up."

Joshua Chamberlain
The Passing of the Armies (p. 37)

Tactics are propelled by circumstances, strategy by circumference. Tactics are only subordinate to strategy on paper. Once put into action, it is tactics, fueled by expediency, that rule the battlefield, military or economic.

TECHNOLOGY'S LIMITS

With the old smoothbore, effective range—that is, the range at which massed infantry fire would hit often enough to be adequately damaging—was figured at just above one hundred yards. I believe it was U. S. Grant himself who remarked that with the old musket a man might shoot at you all day, from a distance of one hundred and fifty yards or more, without even making you aware that he was doing it.

The point of infantry tactics in 1861 was that they depended on this extreme limitation of the infantry's effective field of fire. A column of assault, preparing to attack an enemy position, could be massed and brought forward with complete confidence that until it got to comparatively close range, nothing very damaging could happen to it. From that moment on, everything was up to the determination and numbers of the attackers.

Bruce Catton
America Goes to War: An Introduction to the
Civil War and Its Meaning to Americans Today (p. 15)

A technology's edge is an invisible edge, its obsolescence certain. A failure to understand or appreciate limits to existing technology has sent more organizations into obsolescence than anything else, except poor leadership. Top management generally does not know its own technology, how far to exploit it, or how to enhance its worth. There are only three ways to foster technological health: purchase, modify, or invent—constantly. Joseph Priestly gives fair warning to leaders in regard to technology's limits:

"We are, as it were, laying gunpowder, grain by grain, under the old building of error and superstition, which a single spark may hereafter inflame, so as to produce an instantaneous explosion, in consequence of which that edifice, the erection of which has been the work of ages, may be overturned in a moment and so effectively as that the same foundation can never be built upon again."[18]

When leaders cling to the way they've always done things, a more technologically advanced competitor will let them "shoot . . . all day . . . without even [being] aware [of] it." Clinging to old technologies cripples the effectiveness of organizations unless the leadership can recover in time. Defenders can fight back when challenged. Chances are they will be close, but not quite at their own technology's limits. The mistake comes in believing that a little bit of maneuvering will mean that "nothing very damaging [will] happen." It will! This last-minute posturing only buys time and is usually not enough to move the organization's resources and culture onto a more accelerated technological curve. So protect your technological flanks, embrace relevant technologies with a strategic eye, and refuse to maintain a technology base that approaches obsolescence.

TEAMWORK

True enough, their legs had done it—had "matched the cavalry" as Grant admitted, had cut around Lee's best doings. . . . But other things had "done it," the blood was still fresh upon the Quaker Road, the White Oak Ridge, Five Forks, Farmville, High Bridge, and Sailor's Creek . . .

Joshua Chamberlain
The Passing of the Armies (p. 243)

Refusal to empower teams is facsimile management. The bottom line is—organizations must be team built, but leader led.

TENACITY OF PURPOSE

Grant is not a mighty genius but he is a good soldier with great force of character, honest and upright, of pure purposes . . . His prominent quality is unflinching tenacity of purpose, which blinds him to opposition and obstacles and certainly a great quality in a commander . . . Take him all in all, he is in my judgment the best man the war has yet produced.

Gen. George Meade in Bruce Catton's
Grant Takes Command (p. 408–10)

Tenacity is the passionate refusal of the pull of inertia and the push of resistance. Leaders fail who fail to try. Grant's most "prominent quality [was] unflinching tenacity of purpose, which [blinded] him to opposition and obstacles." He could never be defeated because he never felt defeated within. Even the throat cancer that took his life could not defeat him—it vanquished his body but could not penetrate his tenacity of purpose. Racked with excruciating pain, Ulysses S. Grant finished his memoirs, refusing to give in to the murderous torture of the disease.

UNRUFFLED COMPOSURE

But it was in just such sudden emergencies that General Grant was always at his best. Without the change of a muscle of his face, or the slightest alteration of his voice, he quietly interrogated the officers who brought the reports; then, sifting out the truth from the mass of exaggerations, he gave directions for relieving the situation with marvelous rapidity. General Grant then walked over to his own camp, seating himself on a stool in front of this tent, and lighted a fresh cigar.

Horace Porter
Campaigning with General Grant (Preface)

Grant is at his best when tumult surrounds him, because he is unaffected by it, and though he may issue no single order, his presence at once counteracts panic, it allays fear, it induces confidence. His imperturbable appearance and his inevitable cigar restore a broken line more firmly than a fresh division.

J. F. C. Fuller
The Generalship of Ulysses S. Grant (p. 191)

Unruffled composure controls events. Leaders who face disastrous situations "without a change of muscle of [their] face, or the slightest alteration of [their] voice" electrify performance by adding a sense of confidence and stability that literally mesmerizes those present. Anyone who wants to lead will need that quality in abundance. A sobering thought, isn't it?

UNRUFFLED COMPOSURE RUFFLED

General Meade was an officer of great merit . . . he could execute an order which changed his plans with the same zeal he would have displayed if the plan had been his own. . . . He was brave and conscientious and commanded the respect of all who knew him . . .

He was unfortunately of a temper that would get beyond his control, at times, and make him speak to officers of high rank in the most offensive manner. No one saw this fault more plainly than he himself, and no one regretted it more. This made it unpleasant at times, even in battle, for those around him to approach him even with information.

U. S. Grant
The Personal Memoirs of Ulysses S. Grant (p. 657)

He went on toward Cold Harbor, and on the first day of June saw an army teamster whose wagon was stalled in mud cruelly hitting his horses in the face with the butt end of a whip. "What does this conduct mean, you scoundrel?" Grant demanded. "Stop beating those horses!"

"Well," said the teamster, coolly giving a slap to the face of the wheel horse, "whose driving this team . . . ?"

"I'll show you, you infernal villain!" Grant screamed. He called an officer of the escort and said, "Take this man in charge and have him tied up to a tree for six hours as a punishment . . . "

Gene Smith
Lee and Grant (p. 215)

The best remedy for anger is postponement. Temper is acidic. It burns. Once unleashed, as Meade discovered, it is offensive and regrettable. It leaves emotional stains. Creates resentment. Fertilizes revenge. Grant was a man who felt deeply. He felt for all that lived. He lost his temper rarely, usually when people or animals were mistreated. Can anger, justifiably directed, be righteous? Perhaps. Maybe not. Going ballistic is surrendering to something or someone else, handing over power to it. However, anger, like any other emotion, is a choice. Choose to stay unruffled.

UNVARNISHED LISTENING

<hr>

Like nearly all men who speak little, [Grant] was a good listener.
Horace Porter
Campaigning with General Grant (p. 13)

Make listening one of your highest management priorities.
Speak less and say more. You don't learn anything new when you're
the one doing the talking. Listen carefully so you can be open to
unencumbered awareness. Part of this awareness is listening to circumstance; becoming cognizant of what is really going on; hearing
the nuances, the subtleties of experience. Winston Churchill captured
it when he observed: "Men stumble over the truth from time to time,
but most pick themselves up and hurry off as if nothing happened."[19]

Unvarnished listening is perhaps the single best empowerment tool
available to leaders today.

VISION

Grant has gone down in history as a bludgeon general, a general who eschewed maneuver and who with head down, seeing red, charged his enemy again and again like a bull: indeed an extraordinary conclusion, for no general in this war, not excepting Lee, and few generals in any other war, made greater use of maneuver in the winning of his campaigns, if not of his battles. Without fear of contradiction, it may be said that Grant's object was consistent; strategically it was to threaten his enemy's base of operations, and tactically to strike at the rear, or, failing the rear, at a flank of his enemy's army.

J. F. C. Fuller
The Generalship of Ulysses S. Grant (p. 195)

When Vicksburg surrendered, his next idea was to move on Mobile, in order to establish a base of operations against Georgia and the eastern Confederate States. From Paducah to Appomattox, as we shall see, Grant's strategical plan, upon which all actions were to pivot, was maintained in spite of all difficulties; this in itself constitutes one of the most remarkable cases of concentration of purpose and maintenance of direction to be found in the history of war.

J. F. C. Fuller
The Generalship of Ulysses S. Grant (p. 194)

. . . there is a strength to Grant's narrative that argues against their being overvalued. He could sustain a story through two wars and eleven hundred pages. He had an extraordinary capacity to see certain of his life's experiences with a forbidding wholeness, and could carry that wholeness efficiently to the printed page.

William S. McFeely
Grant: A Biography (p. 510)

A compelling vision is a collision between idea and internal cinema pushed into reality. An effective vision is a statement of unwavering resolve that meets these conditions: It is nontrivial. It has weight. It has teeth. It demands considerably more than hip-pocket interest. It must become gospel. It must convey a precise mission that people in the organization can understand, relate to, believe in, and put into action. It must be an inspiring catalyst for empowerment. It must differentiate the organization in some meaningful way from its competitors in the eyes of the customer. It must be a simply articulated declaration, explaining what business you're in. It must be preached passionately and lived faithfully with unfailing attention to outcome. The vision must be fortified by continuous *try-fail-adjust* cycles that *guarantee* enduring capacity to produce quality products and distinctive service.

WAR

It is probably well that we had the war when we did. We are better off now than we would have been without it, and have made more rapid progress than we otherwise should have made.

Now our republic has shown itself capable of dealing with one of the greatest wars that was ever made, and our people have proven themselves to be the most formidable in war of any nationality.

But this war was a fearful lesson, and should teach us the necessity of avoiding wars in the future.

U. S. Grant
The Personal Memoirs of Ulysses S. Grant (p. 660)

The war was inevitable and, chillingly, [Grant] concluded that it was "probably well that we had the war when we did," since otherwise the prewar particularism of the states would have hindered national growth and we would have been behind the Europeans in world commerce.

William S. McFeely
Grant: A Biography (p. 511)

Grant "understood that he was engaged in a people's war." Once a moral nation like America fully committed itself to the war, victory had to be total. And total victory against other committed Americans could be achieved only if there were more men available for dying on one side than the other.

Adam Badeau in Russell F. Weigley's
The American Way of War: A History of United States Military Strategy and Policy (p. 150)

War is the indecent commerce of governments. It is a global disinfectant poured on the innocent by the guilty. In war, morality is nothing but contraband; force and fraud are virtues. War is anger gone insane. "War," to repeat Grant, is "a fearful lesson, and should teach us the necessity of avoiding wars in the future."

WORTHY OPPONENTS

～⊙～

"You will find," answered Grant, "that the terms as written do not allow this. Only the officers are allowed to take their private property." Lee read over the second page of the letter again. His face showed his wish. His tongue would not go beyond a regretful "No, I see the terms do not allow it; that is clear."

Grant read his opponent's wish, and, with the fine consideration that prevailed throughout the conversation—one of the noblest of his qualities, and one of the surest evidences of his greatness—he did not humiliate Lee by forcing him to make a direct plea for a modification of terms that were generous. "Well, the subject is quite new to me. I will arrange it in this way: I will not change the terms as now written, but I will instruct the officers I shall appoint to receive the paroles to let all the men who claim to own a horse or mule take the animals home with them to work their little farms."

> Douglas Southall Freeman writes of
> Grant's respect for Lee at Appomattox
> *Lee, An Abridgement* (p. 492)

Grant was discovering Virginia and Robert E. Lee not only unrepentant but also willing to bear the heaviest burden he could inflict. He had not expected that. Nor had he expected to find himself admiring his *reprehensible* foe.

> Bruce Catton
> *Grant Takes Command* (p. 235)

Our greatest foes, our greatest adversaries, are within. Leaders who win in highly competitive markets may come to look upon the deaths of their enemies (competitors) with as much regret as they feel for those of their own colleagues, namely, when they miss their existence as witnesses to their continued success. As Grant can attest, one of the most time-consuming activities to endure is dealing with opponents. But feeling at peace with yourself allows you to respect your opponents, and treat them humanely. You may find yourself, like Grant, not "expect[ing] to find [yourself] admiring [your] *reprehensible* foe."

146

GRANT'S ONLY SURRENDER

The following day he was so drowsy that Douglas thought he would die. But he did not die. Not the malnutrition, massive bleeding, or pneumonia would rob the inexorable cancer of its power to destroy. He lasted the night . . . but the morphine was doing its work. The family came downstairs. Julia had already come in to be with her husband. (There were no real last words.) At 8:00 A.M. on July 23, 1885, Ulysses S. Grant died.

William S. McFeely
Grant: A Biography (p. 517)

Take an unconscionably long time to die; you'll be excused. No one's death passes without a witness. Everyone makes some impression, and those closest to the deceased become benefactors of part of the loved one's liberated soul, and become enriched in their humanity. Just like Grant, we all labor constantly against our own cure, since death is the universal remedy for failing flesh.

ENDNOTES

1. Cher Holton, in a personal interview, Nov. 12, 1994.

2. Peggy Anderson and Michael McKees, *Great Quotes from Great Leaders,* 21.

3. Tom Peters and Nancy Austin, *A Passion for Excellence,* 391.

4. Anderson and McKees, *Great Quotes from Great Leaders,* 11.

5. Ibid., 8.

6. Ibid., 17.

7. Edgar F. Puryear, Jr., *19 Stars,* 149.

8. Cher Holton, in a personal interview, Feb. 12, 1995.

9. Excerpts from The Declaration of Independence, Lincoln's Gettysburg Address, and John F. Kennedy's Inaugural Speech, *The Book of Great American Documents,* 5, 75, 87.

10. Oscar Wilde, *3500 Good Quotes for Speakers,* 65.

11. Mark Sanborn, regarding Gen. H. Norman Schwarzkopf, *Teambuilt,* 68.

12. Richard Foster, *Innovation: The Attacker's Edge,* 252.

13. H. Thomas Johnson and Robert S. Kaplan, *Relevance Lost: The Decline and Fall of Management Accounting,* 113.

14. Tom Peters, *Thriving on Chaos,* 244, 246.

15. Eleanor Roosevelt, *The Last Word,* 263.

16. Jean-Paul Sartre, *Being and Nothingness,* Sc 3.

17. Father Theodore Hesburgh, *Time Magazine,* May 1987.

18. Joseph Priestly, *Innovation: The Attacker's Edge,* 370.

19. John-Roger and Peter McWilliams, *Life 101,* 370.

Agassiz, A., ed. *Meade's Headquarters 1863–1865: Letters of Colonel Theodore Lyman from The Wilderness to Appomattox.* Washington, D.C.: Government Printing Office, 1980.

Anderson, Nancy Scott, and Dwight Anderson. *The Generals.* New York: Wings Books, 1987.

Anderson, Peggy, and Michael McKees. *Great Quotes from Great Leaders.* Lombard, Ill.: Celebrating Excellence Publishing, 1990.

Badeau, Adam. *Military History of Ulysses S. Grant,* Vol. 1. New York: Appleton, 1882.

Catton, Bruce. *America Goes to War: An Introduction to the Civil War and Its Meaning to Americans Today.* New York: MJF Books, 1958.

———. *Grant Moves South.* Boston: Little Brown, 1960.

Chamberlain, Joshua. *The Passing of the Armies.* Dayton, Ohio: Morningside Bookshop, 1982.

Church, William C. *Ulysses S. Grant and the Period of National Preservation and Reconstruction.* New York: G. P. Putnam's Sons, 1897.

Coppee, Henry. *Life and Services of U.S. Grant.* Chicago: G. Peterson 1878.

Dowdey, Clifford. *Lee's Last Campaign.* Lincoln, Nebr.: The University of Nebraska Press, 1960.

Flood, Charles Bracelen. *Lee: The Last Years.* Boston: Houghton Mifflin Co., 1981.

Foster, Richard. *Innovation: The Attacker's Edge.* New York: Summit Books, 1985.

Frassanito, William A. *Grant and Lee.* New York: Charles Scribner's Sons, 1983.

Freeman, Douglas Southall. *Lee, An Abridgement* by Richard Harwell. New York: Charles Scribner's Sons, 1961.

Fry, Gen. James B. *Military Miscellanies.* Washington, D.C.: Government Printing Office, 1881.

Fuller, J. F. C. *The Generalship of Ulysses S. Grant.* New York: A Da Capo Paperback, 1929.

———. *Grant and Lee.* Bloomington: Indiana University Press, 1982.

Grant, Ulysses S. *The Personal Memoirs of Ulysses S. Grant.* New York: Konecky & Konecky, 1855.

John-Roger, and Peter McWilliams. *Life 101.* Los Angeles: Prelude Press, 1991.

Johnson, H. Thomas, and Robert S. Kaplan. *Relevance Lost: The Decline and Fall of Management Accounting.* Boston: Harvard Business School Press, 1987.

Johnston, Gen. Joseph. *Leading American Soldiers.* H. Holt and Co., 1907.

Lewis, Lloyd. *Captain Sam Grant.* Boston: Little, Brown & Co., 1950.

Lieberman, Gerald. *3500 Good Quotes for Speakers.* New York: Doubleday, 1983.

McFeely, William S. *Grant: A Biography.* New York: Norton & Company, 1981.

Packard, J. F. *Grant's Tour Around the World, With Incidents of His Journey Through England, Ireland and Scotland.* Philadelphia: Gorton, 1880.

Peters, Tom. *Thriving on Chaos.* New York: Alfred A. Knopf, 1987.

Peters, Tom, and Nancy Austin. *A Passion For Excellence.* New York: Random House, 1982.

Pletcher, David M. *Rails, Mines and Progress: Seven American Promoters in Mexico.* Ithaca, N.Y.: Cornell University, 1958.

Porter, Horace. *Campaigning With General Grant.* New York: Bantam Books, 1991.

Puryear, Edgar F., Jr. *19 Stars.* Novato, Calif.: Presidio Press, 1971.

Sartre, Jean-Paul. *Being and Nothingness, Freedom,* Sct. 3, 1943.

Scott, Robert N. *The War of the Rebellion,* Vol. 3, Official Records February 16, 1862. Washington, D.C.: Government Printing Office, 1880.

Smith, Gene. *Lee and Grant.* New York: Promontory Press, 1984.

Thayer, William M. *From Tannery to the White House: The Life of Ulysses S. Grant.* Boston: H. J. Earle, 1887.

Warner, Carolyn. *The Last Word.* Englewood Cliffs, N.J.: Prentice Hall,1992.

Webb, Ross A. *Benjamin Helm Bristow: Border State Politician.* Lexington, Ky.: University of Kentucky, 1969.

Weigley, Russell F. *The American Way of War: A History of United*

States Military Strategy and Policy. New York: MacMillan, 1973.

Wilson, Vincent J., ed. *The Book of Great American Documents.* Brookeville, Md.: American History Research Associates, 1993.

Wright, Charles W. *A Corporal's Story: Experiences in the Ranks of Company C., 81st Ohio Volunteer Infantry.* Philadelphia: Centennial Press, 1987.

NOTES

NOTES

NOTES

NOTES

NOTES